HABITUDES®

IMAGES
THAT FORM
LEADERSHIP
HABITS &
ATTITUDES

CAREER READY STUDENTS

BY

DR TIM
ELMORE

PUBLISHED IN ATLANTA, GEORGIA BY GROWING LEADERS, INC. (WWW.GROWINGLEADERS.COM)

THE GROWING LEADERS CAREER READY STANDARDS ARE BASED THE CAREER READY PRACTICES, WHICH ARE PART OF THE COMMON CAREER TECHNICAL CORE (WWW.CAREERTECH.ORG/CCTC <HTTP://WWW.CAREERTECH.ORG/CCTC>). THE COMMON CAREER TECHNICAL CORE ARE WHOLLY OWNED AND THE COPYRIGHT HELD BY THE NATIONAL ASSOCIATION OF STATE DIRECTORS OF CAREER TECHNICAL EDUCATION/NATIONAL CAREER TECHNICAL EDUCATION FOUNDATION (NASDCTEc/NCTEF). ANY USE OF THESE STATEMENTS MUST BE ACCOMPANIED BY THE FOLLOWING COPYRIGHT STATEMENT:

"© COPYRIGHT 2012. NATIONAL ASSOCIATION OF STATE DIRECTORS OF CAREER TECHNICAL EDUCATION/NATIONAL CAREER TECHNICAL EDUCATION FOUNDATION (NASDCTEc/NCTEF). ALL RIGHTS RESERVED."

ISBN: 978-0-9960783-5-1

PRINTED IN THE UNITED STATES OF AMERICA

LIBRARY OF CONGRESS CATALOGUING-IN-PUBLICATION DATA

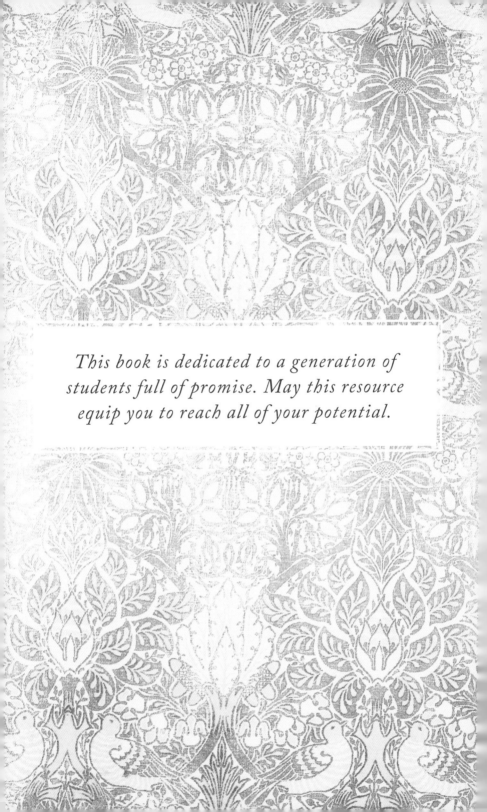

This book is dedicated to a generation of students full of promise. May this resource equip you to reach all of your potential.

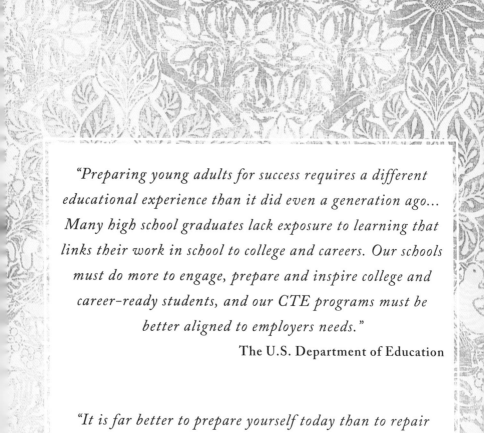

"*Preparing young adults for success requires a different educational experience than it did even a generation ago... Many high school graduates lack exposure to learning that links their work in school to college and careers. Our schools must do more to engage, prepare and inspire college and career-ready students, and our CTE programs must be better aligned to employers needs.*"

The U.S. Department of Education

"*It is far better to prepare yourself today than to repair yourself years into your career.*"

Growing Leaders, 2015

TABLE OF CONTENTS

★

A WORD ABOUT IMAGES

We live in a culture rich with images. We grew up with photographs, TV, movies, video, YouTube and Instagram. We can't escape the power of the visual image—and most of us don't want to.

I've learned over my career that most of us are visual learners. We like to see a picture, not just hear a word. Futurist Leonard Sweet says that images are the language of the 21st century, not words. Some of the best communicators in history taught using the power of the metaphor and image—from Jesus and His parables to Martin Luther King Jr. and his "I Have a Dream" speech, during the Civil Rights movement. "The best leaders," writes Tom Peters, "…almost without exception and at every level, are master users of stories and symbols."

Why?

Because pictures stick. We remember pictures long after words have left us. When we hear a speech, we often remember the stories from that speech, more than the phrases used by the speaker, because they painted a picture inside of us. They communicate far more than mere words. In fact, words are helpful only as they conjure up a picture in our minds. Most of us think in pictures. If I say the word "elephant" to you, you don't picture the letters: e-l-e-p-h-a-n-t. You picture a big gray animal. Pictures are what we file away in our minds. They enable us to store huge volumes of information. There's an old phrase that has stood the test of time: A picture is worth a thousand words. While studying commercial art in college I recognized the power of the image. Now I get to combine the power of teaching leadership truths with the power of pictures. I hope they linger in your mind and heart. I hope you discover layers of reality in them, as you grow. I trust they'll impact you profoundly as they have me.

This book is about becoming "career-ready." Each image represents a standard the U.S. Department of Education has identified as important for you to embrace to experience a successful career. The pictures are designed for you to discuss with a community of people. Each picture contains layers of reality, and your discussion can go as deep as you allow it to go. This book is part of a family of books created to guide you on your leadership journey.

Some sociologists describe this generation as EPIC: Experiential, Participatory, Image-rich and Connected. If that's true, I believe we'll get the most out of resources that furnish us with an image, which sparks a conversation, which leads to an experience. These images will prepare you for life. Each chapter provides you not only with an image, but a handful of discussion questions, a self-assessment and an exercise in which you can participate. Dive in and experience each one of them. My hope is that they become signposts that guide you, and warn you and inform you on your leadership journey.

Dr. Tim Elmore

WHY IS GETTING READY SO IMPORTANT?

This book is not meant to merely engage students on an important topic, it is meant to solve a problem. It's a problem adults didn't see coming for over a decade.

College and career readiness has become a key priority for the education community and the nation at large. Why? According to the Alliance for Excellent Education, our increasingly competitive global economy makes it imperative that more students enter career fields ready to handle significant jobs that are both rewarding and demanding. Unfortunately, universities and businesses have long expressed concerns that a traditional high school education is not adequately preparing students for life after school. This simply means—whether a graduate chooses college or specialized training, most aren't prepared to succeed in these careers. (Carnevale, et al., 2010; Alliance for Excellent Education).

I have long believed in the simple wisdom of preparation. I learned it from my dad, from participation in Boy Scouts, from playing sports and from taking on my first job at twelve years old. This simple wisdom can be summed up in a single phrase:

PREPARING BEATS REPAIRING.

It takes work to prepare. It requires foresight and the ability to delay gratification. I am convinced, however, it requires less work than the drudgery of repairing my life after entering a career unready. I now believe if I don't spend time preparing myself now…I will most certainly end up spending time repairing myself later.

REPAIRING	PREPARING
1. FOCUSES ON THE PAST	1. FOCUSES ON THE FUTURE
2. IT'S ABOUT PATCHING THINGS UP	2. IT'S ABOUT DOING THINGS RIGHT
3. INVOLVES BAD MEMORIES	3. INVOLVES GREAT DREAMS
4. CENTERS ON DAMAGE CONTROL	4. CENTERS ON PLANNING AND READINESS
5. PLAYS DEFENSE	5. PLAYS OFFENSE
6. WE HAVE REGRETS	6. WE ENJOY ANTICIPATION

Reflect for a moment on a time when you encountered a tough challenge and you felt totally unprepared. In that moment, didn't you find yourself wishing you had done a better job getting ready? From time to time, we can "wing it" in those tough moments and somehow get by. Usually, however, we're not fooling anyone. This will certainly be true about our careers. Those who get ready…get ahead.

According to research from Millennial Branding and Beyond.com, Millennials often arrive at job interviews with little information about the company, and recent grads are the least prepared. Over 73 percent of hiring managers said schools are "only somewhat preparing" students for jobs and interviews, and four in ten said students simply arrive on the job unprepared. Further analysis of surveys taken between 2012-2014 report that between 50 and 78 percent of employers who had job openings did not hire recent graduates simply because they weren't prepared for the job. In short, the jobs were ready, but the graduates weren't.

I say it's time to change that. Let's start now.

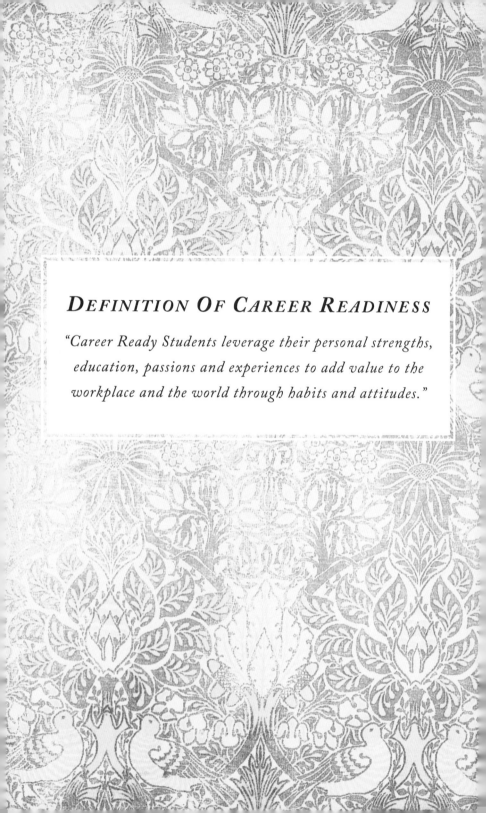

DEFINITION OF CAREER READINESS

"Career Ready Students leverage their personal strengths, education, passions and experiences to add value to the workplace and the world through habits and attitudes."

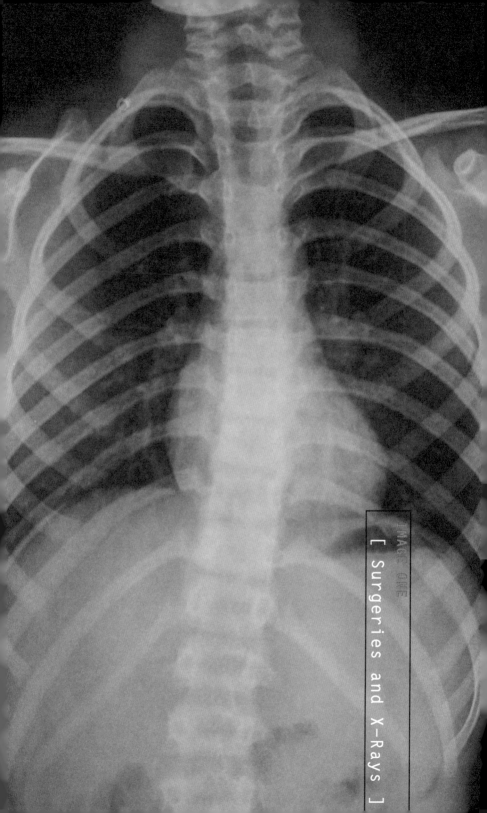

[Surgeries and X-Rays]

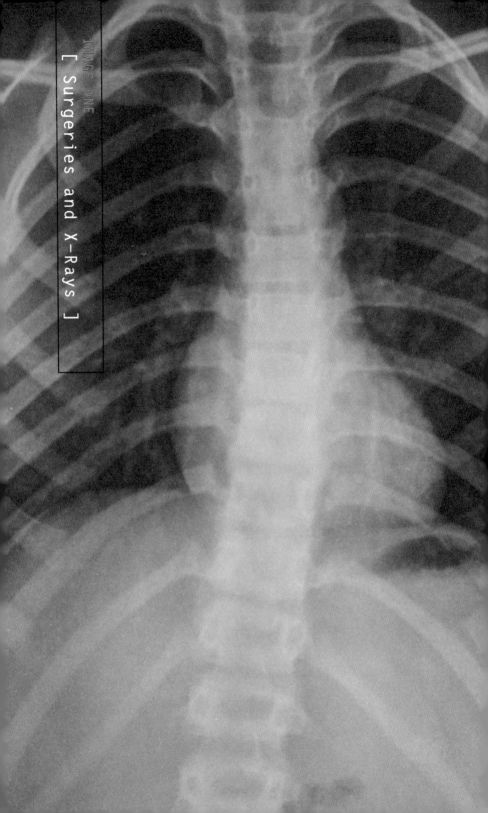

[Surgeries and X-Rays]

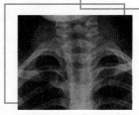

Surgeries and X-Rays

DOCTORS DON'T PERFORM SURGERY ON A BROKEN BONE WITHOUT FIRST TAKING X-RAYS TO DIAGNOSE THE PROBLEM. SIMILARLY, STUDENTS MUST ALWAYS EXAMINE AND DIAGNOSE THEMSELVES BEFORE CHOOSING A CAREER. BEFORE YOU PRESCRIBE AN ACTION, LOOK INSIDE.

One of the saddest stories in American history took place when President James Garfield was shot, on July 2, 1881. The shooter was Charles Guiteau, a crazy man with a pistol in his pocket at a train station. He went on trial for the assassination of President Garfield months later. The pitiful part of the story is that President Garfield didn't die from the gunshot wound; his death was actually due to the misguided treatment of his physician, Dr. Willard Bliss.

Over an eleven-week period of time, Dr. Bliss dug through Garfield's body, searching for the bullet. During that time, Alexander Graham Bell showed up with a new metal detector he'd just created—suggesting that maybe it could help locate the stray bullet. In addition, Joseph Lister had just published his new theory on germs, encouraging doctors to sanitize their hands and instruments before operating on patients. Some of Dr. Bliss' medical team suggested he head this theory, as it seemed to be saving lives around the world.

Unfortunately, Bliss didn't listen to these men. He limited Alexander Graham Bell's search to the right side of Garfield's back because he stubbornly assumed that's where the bullet was. He was wrong. It was on the left side, and they never found it. Further, Bliss felt Joseph Lister's theory about germs was ridiculous. Consequently, he ignorantly explored Garfield's body with dirty utensils and fingers, causing the infection to grow—and eventually kill the president. Essentially, it was Dr. Bliss, the very physician assigned to help Garfield recover, who mortally wounded his patient. As one journalist put it at the time, the physician gave new meaning to the term "Ignorance is bliss."

A Lesson for Us Today

Today, with modern technology and discoveries, doctors recognize the importance of an extensive examination before making a diagnosis. In fact, every patient deserves four outcomes at their doctor's office:

- *A Thorough Examination* (The doctor takes time to look you over)

- *An Accurate Diagnosis* (The doctor evaluates and draws a conclusion)

- *A Proper Prescription* (The doctor matches a solution to the problem)

- *The Best Treatment Available* (The doctor treats or operates on you)

It was tragic that Dr. Bliss didn't provide these four gifts to President Garfield. But let me tell you something that's equally sad. Many students fail to perform them in their own lives and on their future careers. These four items represent different skill sets—and all are needed. Examine. Diagnose. Prescribe. Act. I believe we must develop these skill sets, too, as we peer into the future.

Once you finish school, you will likely enter a full-time job. For many, it will be your first full-time job. My guess is, you don't just want a "job"—you want a career. You want to do something that matches your gifts and passions, a job that allows you to do something that really matters in the world. You want to invest your life in a challenge that energizes you, utilizes your talents and solves a problem.

In order to prepare for a fitting career, you'll have to go through the same steps a doctor does when he or she treats a patient. This Habitude is all about the process of taking X-rays and performing surgeries. The X-rays are about the examination and the diagnosis. The surgery is about the prescription and treatment. Let's apply these steps to your life and see if they'll help prepare you mentally for your upcoming career.

The Purpose of X-Rays

Seven out of every ten Americans will get an X-ray on some part of their body this year. Dentists use them to find cavities; doctors use them to find broken bones or problems in your chest. Before doctors ever perform an operation, they look at an X-ray to diagnose the patient's condition. The information from a diagnostic X-ray could save your life.

Similarly, you'll want to take time to look "inside" yourself, to see what's there. What are your talents? What are your passions? How about your acquired skills? Is there anything wrong? Are there any unhealthy attitudes or emotions you need to address? What do you need to fix?

Ray came on staff to serve as an intern in our office right out of college. He seemed likeable, and eager to be part of our team. After one short month, it became clear he was not ready for work. Although he was a nice guy, he had a poor work ethic, getting distracted with games on his phone and conversations with teammates. He pushed back on some of the guidelines we followed in our office. He wasn't willing to play "team ball" and cooperate on group projects, missed deadlines and wore clothes that weren't appropriate to serve guests who visited. Further, he began to leave for home an hour early each day, oblivious that he was the only one.

When Holly, our vice president confronted him on these behaviors, he just said he had to be his own person; he just wasn't an "eight-hour-a-day" sort of guy. Both Holly and I attempted to help Ray see the adjustments he had to make, but he just wasn't' willing. Consequently, Ray got an early trip back home to mom and dad. What could've been a great experience following graduation turned into a flop.

Ray's story may seem like an exaggeration to you, but millions of young graduates face the same dilemma. They're not self-aware. They don't know their strengths and weaknesses. Many have delusions of grandeur about their careers. In a recent survey of corporate executives, fifty percent of employers could not fill job vacancies because recent graduates lack basic communication and leadership skills. In other words, the jobs are ready—the students aren't. According to the Association of Graduate Recruiters, the number has climbed since 2005. A large employer recently spoke with the Department of Education in Georgia. In essence, he said, "We are not asking graduates about their GPA or their SAT scores. We are hunting for soft skills, communication skills and leadership skills. And we are not finding them."

The Purpose of Surgeries

When a doctor operates on a patient, they actually put into practice what they've diagnosed. It's about more than books and knowledge and theories. The treatment matches the prescription. In the same way, you must act on what you find when you assess yourself. Quite often, students get this wrong. Forty percent say they chose the wrong major in college; the average student changes majors four times. Half of all students quit before they finish. Further, a 2012 university survey found that the top goals for teen students were:

- *To get rich*

- *To get famous*

It's time to get this right. Students must choose career goals that are challenging yet realistic. A great career is about finding your top strengths and putting them to work to solve a real problem in our world. But it all begins by acting on what you know.

Excellent careers require hard work. They rarely just happen. People usually don't fall into an amazing career without sacrifices, initiative and ambition, serving extra hours, developing a great attitude, having a strong work ethic and a hungry mind.

It's all about paying the price once you know what you want.

In 1921, a surgeon named Dr. Evan Kane learned this lesson. He believed he could perform surgery on a patient using only local anesthesia. (Up until then, doctors put patients to sleep even for minor operations.) When he took the idea to his New York hospital board, they decided to let Dr. Kane try this experimental surgery, but told him he'd have to find his own patient. He agreed. The stage was set.

Dr. Kane finally found a patient, and a time and place to perform his historic surgery. On that day, the room was filled with other doctors and nurses waiting to watch him operate. Dr. Kane performed an appendectomy with such great precision that he got a standing ovation from everyone in the room. It was a success.

The year was 1921. The surgeon was Dr. Evan Kane. And the patient that day… was also Dr. Evan Kane. He performed surgery on himself.

When it comes to our careers—you and I must do the same.

THINK IT OVER, WRITE IT DOWN

1. Why do you think students get confused about their career choice?

_____

_____

2. Which of the doctor's procedures is most challenging for you as you look into your future career? (Circle one.)

a. *A thorough examination* (Looking at what's going on inside)

b. *An accurate diagnosis* (Evaluating and drawing a conclusion)

c. *A proper prescription* (Matching an action to what you discover)

d. *The best treatment available* (Taking action steps in the right direction)

3. In your opinion, what's the most exciting part of launching your career?

_____

_____

4. When you think about working in your future career, what are your biggest concerns? What scares you the most? What might cause you to get stuck?

_____

_____

Evaluate Yourself

Below, begin a list of what's "inside" you that would factor into your career choice:

1. Your talents and strengths:

_____

2. Your interests and passions:

_____

3. Community problems that intrigue you:

_____

4. Your past experience:

_____

5. Industries that seem fascinating:

_____

6. Desires that motivate you:

_____

7. Connections you have in your network:

_____

8. Courses or subjects you've taken:

_____

9. What others have affirmed about you:

_____

10. Opportunities in front of you:

_____

Try It Out

Build out the list above on a sheet of paper. Take as much time as you need to respond to each of the ten categories. Expand it. This could be the beginning of an "X-ray" that can guide your discussions and choices as you consider a career. As you reflect on your answers, do you see any trends or patterns? Are there topics you've written down that come up more than once? Do you see common threads?

When you finish, sit down and talk it over with an adult who knows you. What do they agree with on your list? Do they have any additions to the list? Do they disagree with anything you listed? What advice do they have for you?

Now, what "treatment" makes sense? What steps should you take next?

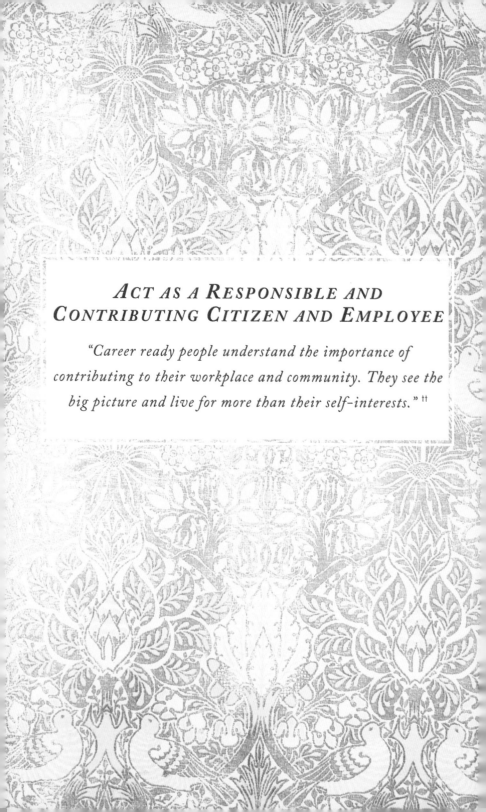

ACT AS A RESPONSIBLE AND CONTRIBUTING CITIZEN AND EMPLOYEE

"Career ready people understand the importance of contributing to their workplace and community. They see the big picture and live for more than their self-interests." [tt]

[Puzzle Pieces and Box Tops]

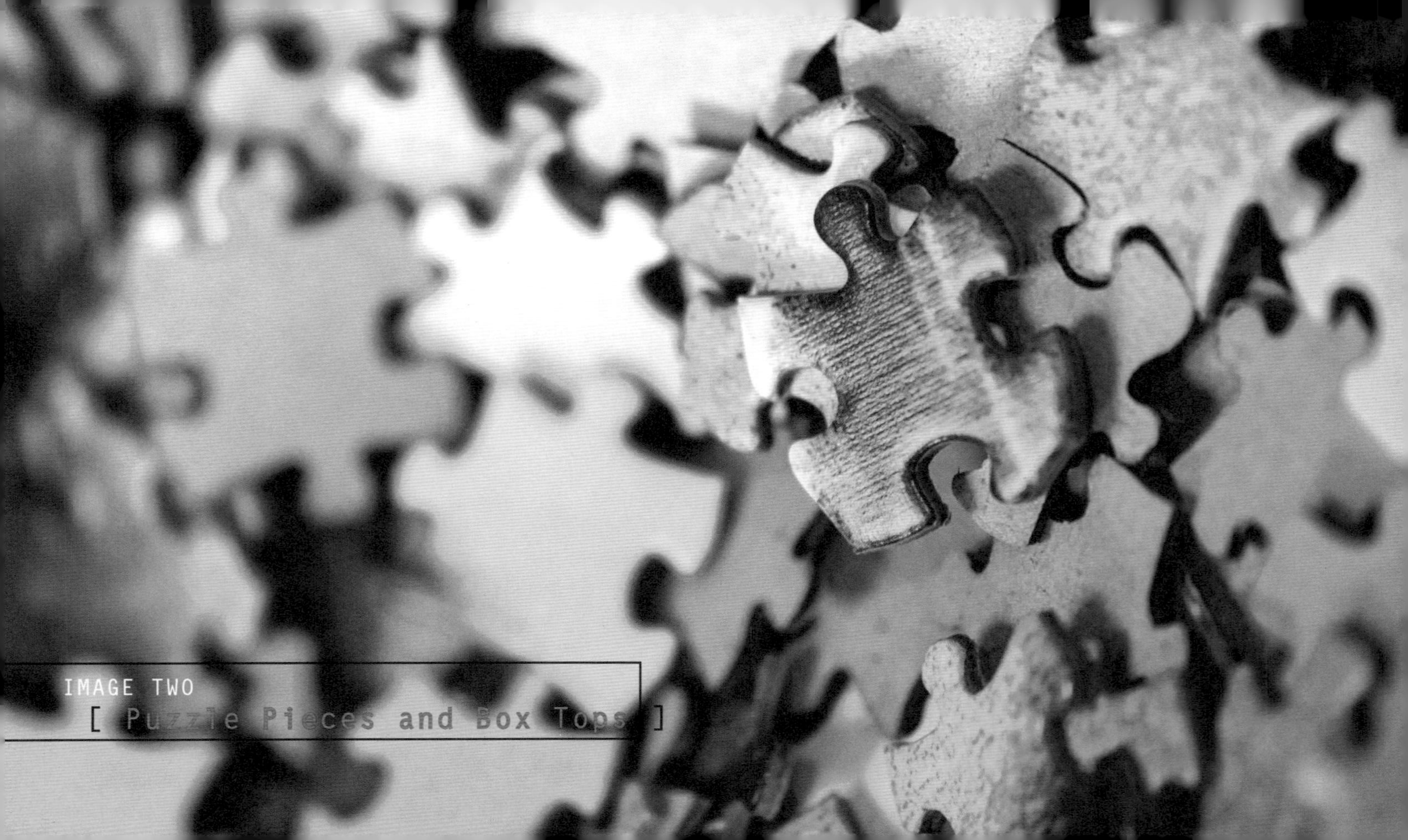

IMAGE TWO

[Puzzle Pieces and Box Tops]

Puzzles Pieces and Box Tops

IT'S VERY DIFFICULT TO PUT A LARGE PUZZLE TOGETHER WITHOUT THE BOX TOP. WHY? BECAUSE THE BOX OFFERS THE BIG PICTURE. IN YOUR CAREER, YOU'LL PLAY A PIECE OF THE PUZZLE, BUT YOU MUST SEE BEYOND YOURSELF. BEING READY FOR A CAREER MEANS MORE THAN IMPROVING YOURSELF. IT MEANS SEEING THE BIGGER PICTURE OF PLAYING A ROLE AT WORK AND IN YOUR COMMUNITY.

A few years ago, artist Royce B. McClure was asked to take on a huge project. He was to design a jigsaw puzzle that would include a breathtaking 24,000 pieces, reaching more than five feet in height and over fourteen feet in width. It was called "Life—The Great Challenge." When it was finished, Guinness World Records officially recognized it as the largest commercial jigsaw puzzle in the world.

Later, students at the University of Economics in Ho Chi Minh, Vietnam, set a new jigsaw puzzle record on September 24, 2011—creating a puzzle with 551,232 pieces! It expanded to over forty-eight feet tall and more than seventy-six feet wide. It was produced at the Phu Tho Stadium because it was so big. How incredible.

Can you imagine putting that puzzle together?

You remember learning to put puzzles together as a young kid, don't you? Consider a jigsaw puzzle for a minute. Usually it contains one big picture made up of hundreds of tiny pieces. Each piece is necessary to create the picture, but no piece can paint the entire picture. This is why puzzles always come in a box with a picture on the top. The box top illustrates what the puzzle should look like when it's finished. Without the box top, it's almost impossible to assemble the puzzle properly. In fact, the bigger the puzzle, the more we need the box top!

The fact of the matter is, in our jobs we are much like this. Workplaces resemble puzzles. We each hold a piece of the puzzle. The full picture doesn't form without everyone playing their part. At the same time, each piece is incomplete without the others. Each team member needs the others. As the saying goes, no man is an island. The bottom line is this—if we are like pieces of the puzzle, then:

- We'd better find out what piece of the puzzle we're designed to play.

- We'd better see the big picture so we can get beyond ourselves.

Nathan never worked a job until he graduated from college. By that time, he was pretty full of himself. He had a degree and had graduated magna cum laude. He'd been at the top of his class. Work, however, was very different from school. He continued to think the same way he'd thought all along—it was all about him, his good grades, his awards, his personal playing time and his own progress. He never really got the big picture—that success was about everyone working well together and achieving the mission as a team. Unfortunately, even though he was smart, he became a liability rather than an asset to his employer. Nathan was let go within a year.

The truth is, our perspective will impact our performance. What you focus on expands. If you don't see the big picture, you won't practice a big-picture lifestyle. Eventually, less talented, even less intelligent people pass you by, because they act in light of the box top as they play their individual piece.

In a different Habitudes book, I mention a speech by President John F. Kennedy. In 1961, President Kennedy shared his goal to put a man on the moon before the end of the decade. At the time he cast this vision, the US didn't even have the technology to do it. However, his idea was infectious. Immediately, the team at NASA focused their energies on this monumental mission. Staff members who for years had felt like "a piece of furniture" began to display unusually strong performance—all because of this vision. It turned average workers into extraordinary workers. To this day, NASA has this performance leap on record. Staff teamed up to land a man on the moon.

What many don't know is that a year later President Kennedy visited NASA to check on their progress. Walking the halls, he accidentally ventured into a storage room. When he entered the room, he saw a custodian with a broom. Kennedy reached out to shake his hand and asked what his job was. The custodian paused, then smiled and replied, "I'm putting a man on the moon, Mr. President."

I love it. The custodian got it. He saw the box top.

The Advantage You Gain...

When people grasp the "box top," vision they often perform beyond their normal capacity. Huge projects invite superior performance. In fact, I've noticed the following advantages occur when I embrace the big picture:

1. I gain a deeper satisfaction being a part of something bigger then "me."

2. I help other people benefit, who may not have done so without my help.

3. I accomplish something far greater than I would have been able to do alone.

This principle is all about "we" instead of "me." I don't know your past. You may or may not have ever been taught to think this way. It's always better. Legendary UCLA coach John Wooden once said, "Individuals win trophies, but teams win championships." All great players will tell you they'd rather win a championship than an MVP trophy. There's something about being a part of a project or an organization that inspires us to go beyond our own selfish interests.

This requires you to look outward beyond your own world. You must see how your actions affect the future of others. It's like seeing through a *telescope*—far out into the world beyond—instead of a *microscope*, where you only see the details in front of you. How about you? Do you see beyond your own personal interests? Putting a puzzle together requires us to look at the box top first, to make sense of the ultimate goal. Only then can you place your piece accurately.

It's amazing how we benefit personally…by focusing on others. It's strange. If we do this at work, our boss tends to notice us and value us more. We gain opportunities that selfish people don't. Other team members actually want to be around us, because we're not self-absorbed. Everyone gets better, including us.

The Result?

When you can see beyond your own life, and bigger than what you alone can pull off, it will transform you. And that's when the benefits show up. Years ago, a group of mountain climbers began freezing in the snow. They ran out of food and feared dying, and that's when one of their team members fainted. One climber pondered how they could carry their unconscious friend, but the rest insisted they continue their descent. They'd surely die if they tried to carry their friend. So the rest of the group continued on as the single climber stayed behind and hoisted his friend onto his back. An hour later—the single climber came upon his teammates. They were lying in the snow, having frozen to death. He, however, remained alive, as he had stayed warm carrying his friend on his back. Getting beyond himself… had actually saved his life.

So it is with our lives.

Think It Over, Write It Down

1. Why do you think most people are all about "me"? Why are we so self-absorbed?

_____

_____

2. Can you name an experience where you saw the power of seeing the big picture?

_____

_____

3. If you were starting a new job, what are some specific behaviors that would show that you see the big picture and are willing to make sacrifices for the organization?

_____

_____

EVALUATE YOURSELF

On a scale of one to ten, circle how you naturally tend to think about your life:

1	2	3	4	5	6	7	8	9	10
I tend to think of myself first						I tend to see the big picture			

1	2	3	4	5	6	7	8	9	10
I look out for my best interests						I tend to sacrifice for the team			

1	2	3	4	5	6	7	8	9	10
In a job interview, I think of what I'll gain						I think of how I can add value			

TRY IT OUT

Think of an area in your life where you tend to think of yourself first. Be honest. We are all selfish from time to time. Now—consider what project you could launch that would not only benefit others, but also help you see the big picture. For example, what if you assembled a small team of students and decided to fix up a vacant lot or some area of your community where things are falling apart? You could even help an elderly person mow their lawn, rake leaves or trim shrubs. Find a place where you could work together on a project that requires a group to pull off results.

For years, Kennesaw Mountain High School students have hosted a special prom dance. It's not for themselves, but for special education students at a nearby school. These kids, who are mentally disabled or somehow handicapped, are escorted through the gym and served by KMHS teens. Kennesaw Mountain students even invite the kids to dance with them. It is a very powerful experience.

When you finish, sit down and talk it over. What were the benefits to you? How about others on the team? How about the one who received the work you did?

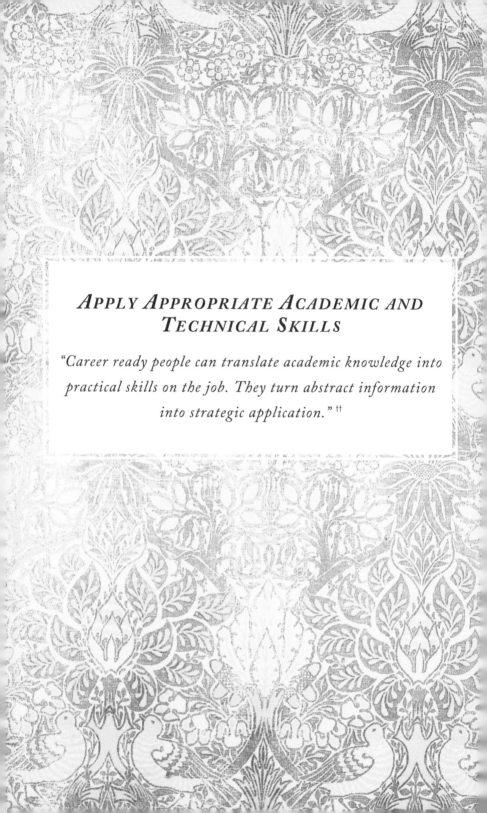

APPLY APPROPRIATE ACADEMIC AND TECHNICAL SKILLS

"Career ready people can translate academic knowledge into practical skills on the job. They turn abstract information into strategic application." [††]

Kitchens and Restaurants

Kitchens and Restaurants

KITCHENS AND RESTAURANTS ARE BOTH ABOUT PREPARING GOOD FOOD. THE DIFFERENCE? IN A RESTAURANT, YOU SIT, AND SOMEONE BRINGS THE FOOD TO YOU. IN A KITCHEN, YOU READ A RECIPE AND MAKE THE FOOD YOURSELF. KNOWLEDGE ISN'T ENOUGH. ACADEMIC AND TECHNICAL SKILLS SHOULD COMPLEMENT EACH OTHER. INFORMATION MUST LEAD TO APPLICATION.

When I was growing up, my family ate most of our meals at home. Mom was a great cook—and seemed to enjoy making roast beef, fried chicken, spaghetti, tacos, salads, pork chops…you name it. Going out to a restaurant was…well, a special treat.

Today, it seems people eat out more often than we did decades ago. There are more restaurants; food is prepared faster than ever, and we are busier than ever. One survey by Groupola.com reports that people ate out sixty-three percent more in 2010 than the year before. Many just don't seem to have time to cook as much at home. Why do that when a professional chef can do it for you? Right?

Today my family loves eating out. We are part of this culture that cooks less at home and eats out more often. Because I travel quite a bit, I find myself eating out on the road regularly, too. Over time, I've noticed there are three kinds of restaurants:

1. *Sit down and place your order with a waiter.*
   This is the traditional restaurant. All the customer does is sit at a table and make a request. There's no contact with the mess in the kitchen.

2. *Sit down and watch a chef prepare your meal on a grill.*
   This is done at hibachi restaurants; observing the meal preparation by a "pro" is all part of the experience.

3. *Walk in and do it yourself—customers take the food they want.*
   This happens in restaurants where diners want to participate in the meal preparation; this could be anything from a salad bar to a dessert bar to a hot buffet.

The first kind is most popular. All of the work is done by professionals. In the third kind, the customer is more involved, but it's still limited. The food is ready and the customer is supervised. It's hard to go wrong. It is still not like cooking in your own kitchen.

This illustrates another truth about life and careers. We have grown up in a world where many of our needs are met by a professional. We take our car into a service station to get the oil changed or have it washed. We take our nice clothes to a dry cleaner. We call a plumber to repair our pipes or an electrician to fix our heater. Some even pay to have their lawns mowed or trees trimmed. None of this is bad— but it's important to note that we rely on others and their skills to survive. We may know a lot about cars or clothes or heaters, but if our knowledge hasn't become an actual skill, it does us little good. To become valuable, people must connect knowledge with skills and abilities. Sooner or later, the stuff you read in a book has to be translated into action. It isn't enough to be "good" at ordering food at a restaurant. We must learn to cook a meal in a kitchen.

AARON AND AUSTIN

Let me introduce you to two students—Austin and Aaron. Both made good grades in high school, but they were very different as they launched their careers. Austin was proud to carry a 4.0 GPA into his first job interview following high school. He was the valedictorian of his school. This made him confident enough to say in the interview, "I'll be supervising a team within twelve months." Unfortunately, his confidence didn't translate into performance. Because he had no experience, he hadn't developed any skills. By the time he reached his ninety-day job review, he was failing on the job. His boss had to let him go. He's now living at home with his parents.

Aaron was also a good student but knew he had to get some experience in a job. So all through his teen years, he found work. Because he wanted to go into hotel management, he got jobs in hospitality, waited tables at cafes, served as a bellhop and even worked on the custodial staff at a hotel. During his college years, he interviewed for a job and was hired immediately. Upon Aaron's graduation, he never had to look for a place to launch his career. He was already in it. He went full-time right out of college. Aaron's scenario is excellent…but far too rare.

ARE YOU READY?

According to one employer survey, somewhere between one third and one half of the job openings for entry-level employees (recent graduates) continue to go unfilled each year. In other words, the jobs were ready—but the graduates weren't. Youth are now three times more likely to be unemployed than their parents.

According to social scientists, this has become more than an economic issue—it's a social and psychological one as well. We cannot survive an economic recession while at the same time producing graduates who haven't been prepared for the working world. Part of the problem is this:

- *Students today are over-exposed to information earlier than they're ready.*

- *Students are under-exposed to real-life experience later than they're ready.*

This over-exposure/under-exposure can produce both arrogance and anxiety. The answer? Just like in a college science class—our learning needs a "lecture" and a "lab." In other words, we need instruction from a teacher or mentor, but we also need to practice what we've heard. That's when real learning takes place.

I want you to imagine a scenario. Suppose you were my supervisor at work and you had to take a trip overseas. You left me in charge, but said you would message me every day on Facebook and give me the instructions I'd need to manage the team. Weeks later, you return…and you're stunned. Our workplace is a mess. Trash is all over, and stacks of work are piled everywhere. Nothing seems to have been done. Finally, you walk to the back room, and there I am…with our team playing video games.

"What are you doing?" you exclaim. "Didn't you get my messages?"

"Oh yeah," I reply with a smile. "We got them and loved reading them. In fact, they were so good, we made a little book out of them, and have studied them each day. Some of us even memorized paragraphs from your messages. They're awesome!"

"But didn't you know I wanted you to implement what I requested?" you ask.

"Implement? I didn't realize you wanted us to actually do something."

My point is simple. This scenario is ridiculous because work is about skills, not just knowledge. It's about application, not just information. That's the power of a kitchen over a restaurant. It's one thing to order food in a cafe or watch the Food Network on television. It's a totally different thing to actually enter the kitchen and apply what you've just seen. Anyone can be a consumer in a restaurant. What we need are cooks who can actually prepare the food themselves. Are you just a customer or a cook? Are you merely a consumer or a contributor?

Think It Over, Write It Down

1. Why is it so hard to move from information to application (or practice)?

_____

_____

2. Do you know students who are anxious about starting their career? Why are they?

_____

_____

3. Why do you think most teens don't work a regular job?

_____

_____

4. If you were interviewing for a job, what skills do you have that you'd highlight?

_____

_____

EVALUATE YOURSELF

On a scale of one to ten, evaluate yourself and circle your honest answer:

STATEMENT:	Seldom									Always
I apply the information I learn.	1	2	3	4	5	6	7	8	9	10

	Not Really									Definitely
I have work experience in a job.	1	2	3	4	5	6	7	8	9	10

	Yes									No
I've developed skills for a career.	1	2	3	4	5	6	7	8	9	10

Try It Out

Think of an industry where you're interested in building a career. In fact, think of two or three career areas you might want to enter. Jot them down. Next, follow up on the list below to actually apply some skills to your interest:

1. What entry-level job could you get that may prepare you to advance in this area?

2. Who do you know who works in this field, who could serve as an informal mentor?

3. How could you gain insights into this career by researching books and websites?

4. Which activities are you currently involved in that will help you build key skills?

5. When could you get started on your preparation?

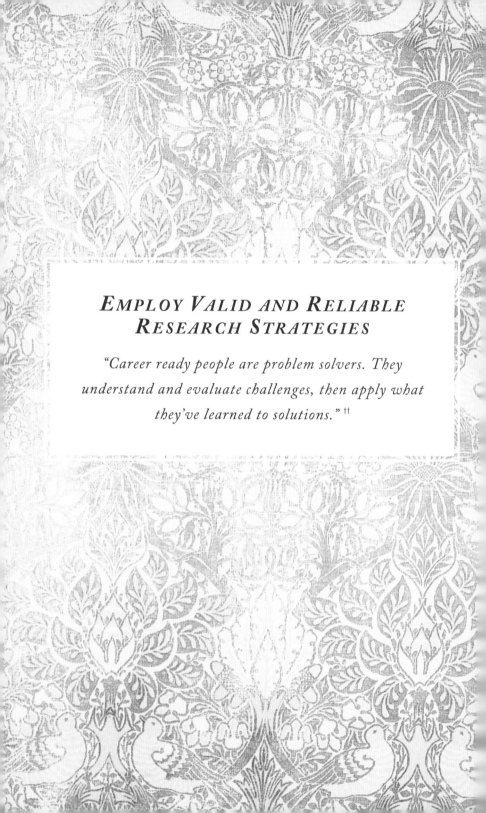

EMPLOY VALID AND RELIABLE RESEARCH STRATEGIES

"Career ready people are problem solvers. They understand and evaluate challenges, then apply what they've learned to solutions." [††]

IMAGE FOUR

[Obstacle Course]

IMAGE FOUR
[Obstacle Course]

Obstacle Course

THE COMPETITION FOR JOBS TODAY IS FIERCE. PEOPLE WHO CAN RECOGNIZE PROBLEMS AND SOLVE THEM ARE THE MOST VALUABLE TEAM MEMBERS. LIKE AN OBSTACLE COURSE, WE MUST WEAVE OUR WAY THROUGH HURDLES AND OVER WALLS TO REACH OUR GOAL. THEY'RE LIKE TESTS WE MUST PASS. VALUABLE LEADERS LEARN TO SOLVE PROBLEMS TO BETTER SERVE PEOPLE.

Recently, our Growing Leaders team visited a retreat center for a day of team building. It was a blast to climb poles, run relays and see how fast we could build structures with strange-looking objects. It was hilarious to watch full-grown adults engage in problem-solving exercises in the great outdoors.

One of the most noticeable areas on the campground was an obstacle course. It had zip lines, walls to overcome, cones to maneuver, mud to crawl through, tires to jump in, and, of course, a fifteen-foot pole for teams to climb and stick a flag on once they finished the course. It's exhilarating just to watch people experience it.

Some people, however, give up too soon. On almost every team, a person or two just decides it's not worth it. It's too hard. They're not athletic enough or they don't want to break a sweat or ruin their hair. You know what I mean. And while there's nothing wrong with these team members, they never experience what others do who actually finish the obstacle course. It's all theory to them.

LIFE'S AN OBSTACLE COURSE

In many ways, obstacle courses are a great picture of life and work. Almost every day, there are problems that need to be solved. In fact, I believe the key to nearly every job is the ability to solve problems so you can better serve people. The trouble is, we find it easy to see problems as an enemy. We complain when stuff gets too hard or we cannot find the solution quickly. We need to remember—work is like an obstacle course that must be finished. The adventure and the inner reward come only when we approach it with this attitude. If we try to take shortcuts, we are the ones who lose in the end.

page 29

As a teen, I ran on our school track team. I was a distance runner, and I prepared for races with my teammate Tom. I will never forget one afternoon when we were attempting to qualify for the conference track meet the following week. Tom noticed our coach turn away to talk to a faculty member; immediately, he ducked behind the bleachers and hid while the rest of us continued to run the next two laps. Finally, on the final lap, Tom was well-rested and rejoined us. By then, he had the energy to finish first and qualify for the meet. The rest of us were ticked off. He had obviously taken a shortcut to his goal and didn't deserve to compete. Justice prevailed, however, at the conference meet. Halfway through the race, Tom never got his second wind, and he stopped running. He was "out of gas." He vomited and came close to dehydration. I felt badly for Tom—but I know why it happened. He'd never really paid the price to be in that race. He'd taken a shortcut.

According to a national survey of corporate executives, one of the top three qualities organizations look for in new job candidates is problem-solving skills. They report that if potential employees are good at spotting problems and solving them, they are valuable team members and often draw larger salaries. Further, they are very difficult to replace. There are three ingredients in the problem-solving recipe:

1. You must see and clearly define the problem. This requires perspective.

2. You must develop a set of options for solutions. This requires creativity.

3. You must find ways to implement the best solution. This requires tenacity.

All of this demands some good, old-fashioned resiliency. To be resilient means you have the ability to bounce back if your first solution doesn't work. You have the optimism and energy to fail, get back up and try again. I love how Elizabeth Edwards defined it: "Resilience is accepting your new reality, even if it's less good than the one you had before. You can fight it, you can do nothing but scream about what you've lost, or you can accept that and try to put together something that's good."

Mike Norton writes, "Never say that you can't do something, or that something seems impossible, or that something can't be done, no matter how discouraging or harrowing it may be; human beings are limited only by what we allow ourselves to be limited by: our own minds. We are each the masters of our own reality; when we become self-aware to this: absolutely anything in the world is possible."

BECOMING SOLUTION-MINDED

The better you are at coming up with solutions, the more valuable you become to a team or an organization. For twenty years, I worked with Dr. John Maxwell, an executive, leadership author and speaker. John had a rule—we could never come to him complaining about a problem unless we also brought with us three ideas for solutions. This kept us on our toes and helped us maintain a positive attitude.

Each of us got very creative at fixing dilemmas. In fact, we used to compare it to the difference between a pocketknife and a Swiss Army knife. A pocketknife has a single blade and is good for simple cutting needs. A Swiss Army knife has all kinds of options to it. In addition to the main blade, its most common features are a smaller second blade, tweezers, toothpick, corkscrew, can opener, bottle opener, flat-head screwdriver, Phillips-head screwdriver, nail file, scissors, wood saw, file, hook, magnifying glass, ballpoint pen, fish scaler, pliers, and key ring. Needless to say, a Swiss Army knife is more valuable than a pocketknife. Similarly, when it comes to problem solving, a person who brings lots of options is more valuable than a person with just one. By focusing on the goal, solutions arise more quickly than complaints.

Case in point: Charles Darrow set a goal in the 1920s to be a millionaire. En route to this goal, however, the stock market crashed in November 1929. He and his wife lost almost everything. It was the biggest problem they'd ever faced. But Charles and his wife were problem solvers. Instead of giving up, they decided to do something every day to keep their eye on their goal. They began playing an imaginary game, conversing about what they would do if they had a million dollars. To keep it interesting, they eventually created play money, and later a board, dice, cards and hotels...and by 1932, Charles Darrow had created a game you likely have in your closet today: Monopoly. Right in the heat of the Great Depression. What's more, in 1935, Parker Brothers bought the game from Mr. Darrow. Do you know how much they paid him for it? One million dollars.

Problems are everywhere, and if you can solve them—you'll likely never be out of a job. While failure is part of life, giving up shouldn't be. Just ask R. H. Macy. He failed seven times before his store in New York caught on. Novelist John Creasey received 753 rejection slips before he published the first of his 564 books. Thomas Edison was thrown out of school very early on because the teacher decided he couldn't do the work. When J. K. Rowling wrote her first Harry Potter book, it was turned down twelve times. And when Bob Dylan performed at a high school talent show, his classmates booed him off the stage. Eventually, these people became wildly successful—because they didn't give up when they faced obstacles.

What will you do with your next obstacle course?

THINK IT OVER, WRITE IT DOWN

1. Why is it so easy to see problems and so hard to see solutions?

_____

_____

2. In which of the three ingredients in this chapter—perspective, creativity, tenacity—are you the strongest? Which of the three is most challenging for you?

_____

_____

3. In a job interview, how would you describe your problem-solving skills?

_____

_____

Evaluate Yourself

Place an X on the dotted line to indicate your most accurate response:

1. When something goes wrong, I'm able to naturally identify the root problem.

Agree -- Disagree

2. I enjoy problem solving and often come up with several solutions to a problem.

Agree -- Disagree

3. I seldom get frustrated when a problem takes a long time to solve.

Agree -- Disagree

Try It Out

Get together with a group of two other students. Decide on a current, real-life problem that exists on your campus, or imagine you are in charge of solving a problem in your community. Next, walk through the three steps of problem solving:

1. Clearly define the problem that must be solved.

2. Identify at least three possible solutions.

3. Walk through the steps to implement the best solution.

Afterward, discuss how things went. Where were you strong and weak?

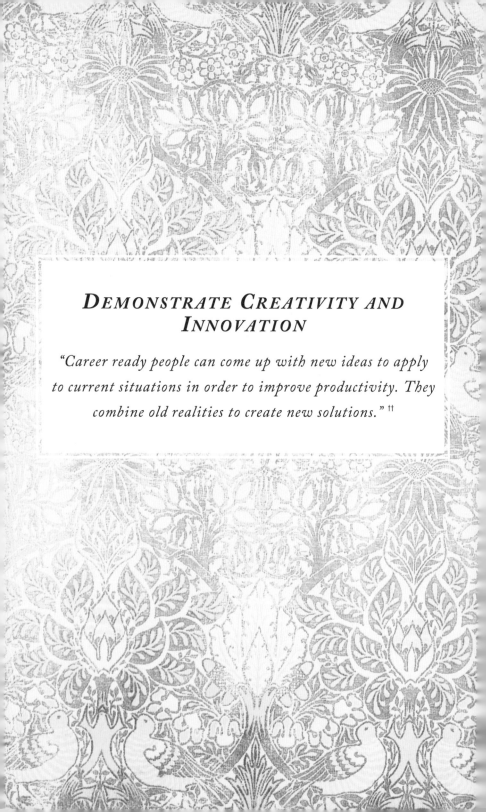

DEMONSTRATE CREATIVITY AND INNOVATION

"Career ready people can come up with new ideas to apply to current situations in order to improve productivity. They combine old realities to create new solutions." [††]

Bikes and Birds

IT WAS A BICYCLE AND A BIRD THAT ENABLED MANKIND TO LEARN TO FLY. TWO EXISTING IDEAS THAT HELPED CREATE A NEW ONE. THIS IS THE NEED OF THE HOUR IN THE 21ST-CENTURY WORKPLACE. INNOVATION THAT COMES FROM ORDINARY PEOPLE WHO RECOGNIZE HOW TO TAKE TWO OR MORE REALITIES AND GENERATE NEW AND BETTER IDEAS.

In 1899, Wilbur Wright wrote a letter of request to the Smithsonian Institute for information about flight experiments. He and his brother Orville had come up with an idea for their first aircraft from a most unusual set of circumstances.

The Wright Brothers were bicycle shop owners who loved improving how people enjoyed smooth transportation from one spot to another on two wheels. They understood a bike backwards and forwards and were always trying to enhance its design. Over time, Orville and Wilbur spent increasing hours observing birds in flight. In fact, they read everything they could get their hands on about birds. They noticed that birds soared into the wind and that the air flowing over the curved surface of their wings created lift. Birds change the shape of their wings to turn and maneuver. The Wrights believed that they could use this technique to obtain roll control by warping, or changing the shape of, a portion of the wing.

Six years earlier a German engineer, Otto Lilienthal, had died after attempting human flight. Orville and Wilbur figured that maybe the answer to successful flight could be found in the design of both a bird and a bike. Later that year, they constructed their first plane—a small, biplane glider flown as a kite to test a solution for controlling the craft by wing warping. It worked. Over the next three years, Wilbur and his brother Orville designed a series of gliders, drawing from the design of a bicycle, then placing moving wings and tail on it, like a bird. In December 1903, they finally did it. Orville took their "Flyer" for a twelve-second ride over Kitty Hawk, North Carolina. This was the first successful, powered, piloted flight in history.

Few would doubt that Orville and Wilbur Wright were creative geniuses. What we tend to forget is that their idea for an airplane was simply a combination of two existing realities: a bird and a bike. This is a secret that each of us should know. Every new generation must create new realities, but the best creativity usually lies in combining two or more existing realities to generate an original. In one sense, the Wright brothers had simply designed a flying bike.

Steve Jobs brilliantly declared, "Creativity is just connecting things." While we often think of great innovators as people who dream up ideas out of nothing, Steve Jobs was explaining that the freshest ideas are usually merely new combinations of stuff that already exists. Under Jobs' leadership, for example, Apple didn't invent MP3 players or tablet computers—they just made them better, with features that were new to the category. Similarly, Johannes Gutenberg worked with wine presses, then simply applied his knowledge of wine presses to a printing machine able to mass-produce words instead of wine. Street performers Daniel Gauthier and Guy Laliberte turned their knowledge of the circus, gymnastics and theater into a splendid new category of entertainment: Cirque du Soleil. It was three old ideas that originated a new one.

Here's the good news: If you're young, it's likely you already value creativity. In general, most students enjoy "new stuff" and love creative people and environments that allow them to utilize their ingenuity.

In addition, students also love connection. They love to stay connected socially (to friends) and technologically (to ideas). Research reveals teens are disconnected from people and technology only one hour in a twenty-four-hour day. Like creativity, connectivity is often your "middle name." What your career will need from you is to not only learn the ropes of the working world you're about to enter, but also to exercise these two elements—creativity and connectivity. Connect ideas and people to create new ideas and innovations.

At fifteen years old, Jack Andraka created a new diagnostic test for pancreatic cancer that is twenty-eight times faster, 26,000 times less expensive and over a hundred times more sensitive than the current diagnostic tests. If that's not enough, the test works for ovarian and lung cancer as well. Not bad for a kid who doesn't even have his driver's license. How did he do it?

In school, Jack displayed a curious and hungry mind. It sent him on a hunt to figure out current ways the medical world tested for cancer and how to improve that testing. His solution came to him during biology class when he was secretly reading an article about nanotubes while his teacher spoke about antibodies. Jack said the two ideas came together in his head and he combined them to create the test.

It's all about bikes and birds.

So What Do We Do?

As you prepare to enter your career, you'll need to be both consistent and creative. This means you'll have to learn to produce results in a steady fashion, even if you don't love every moment of your day. At the same time, you must capture moments that allow you to create something new. Focus on creativity and connection when given the opportunity. Here are my seven rules for cultivating creativity in people:

1. *Find opportunities to work in communities. Get connected.*

2. *Ensure people bring diverse experiences and gifts to those communities.*

3. *Identify the clear objective, but approach solutions with all-new methods.*

4. *Understand the "why" behind the project before you get to the "what."*

5. *Provide stimulation without too much structure. Few rules. Free thinking.*

6. *Give and receive affirmation (belief in others) and consistent feedback.*

7. *Prepare for answers that are "out of the box." Don't shoot them down instantly.*

In these environments, it's amazing how many new ideas spring up. For decades, the company 3M has offered its employees about one day a week to work on anything they want to. They can work in teams or alone, but either way the goal is to generate new ideas. Some of their best products have come from those days, including the Post-it Notes you probably have on your desk. The company Google does the same thing—it gives its teams twenty percent of every week to get creative. The only rule is—you have to work on something you believe is worthwhile. Once again, some of Google's most famous ideas have come from that "free time." Do you realize that Gmail was actually invented on one of those creative days?

The key is to stop making excuses by saying "I'm not very creative." Everyone can be creative, but they must get used to thinking new thoughts by connecting often unrelated ideas to solve a problem. And that's where to get started—with a problem. Your greatest motivation to create comes when you face a problem to solve. Jacob Schick invented the electric razor while living in freezing temperatures. He hated putting a blade to his face. Charles Kettering invented the electronic ignition when he hurt himself cranking up an old automobile. Neither Schick nor Kettering was a specialist in razors or cars—which may have been the key to their creativity. They weren't bound by old ideas in that industry. The cotton gin was invented by Eli Whitney...who was an attorney and tutor. Kodachrome was invented by two musicians. The continuous steel casting process was invented by a watchmaker.

So—what will you create from your own bikes and birds?

Think It Over, Write It Down

1. Why do people get stuck doing things the way they've always done them?

_____

_____

2. In what situations do you find you're most creative? What helps you get creative?

_____

_____

3. Have you ever come up with a new idea by connecting a few existing ones?

_____

_____

4. In a job interview, would you describe yourself as a creative person? Why?

_____

_____

Evaluate Yourself

Place an X on the dotted line to indicate your most accurate response:

1. When you get stuck on a problem, do you get frustrated or creative?

Frustrated --Creative

2. Where do you need to grow the most in your life when it comes to creativity?

Familiar places--Unfamiliar places

Try It Out

Henry Ford, the man who invented the automobile, said, "I never invented anything new." Think of a product or a service that a company provides that you think could be improved upon. Next, either on your own or with a team of friends, walk through the list of seven rules for creativity above. Find ways to connect existing ideas to generate a new one. Think outside the box. Write everything down. Once you come up with some ideas, vote on the best one and begin to lay out your game plan, as if you were asked by your supervisor at work to create a new product or service.

How did you do? What did you come up with? Share it with your class or teacher.

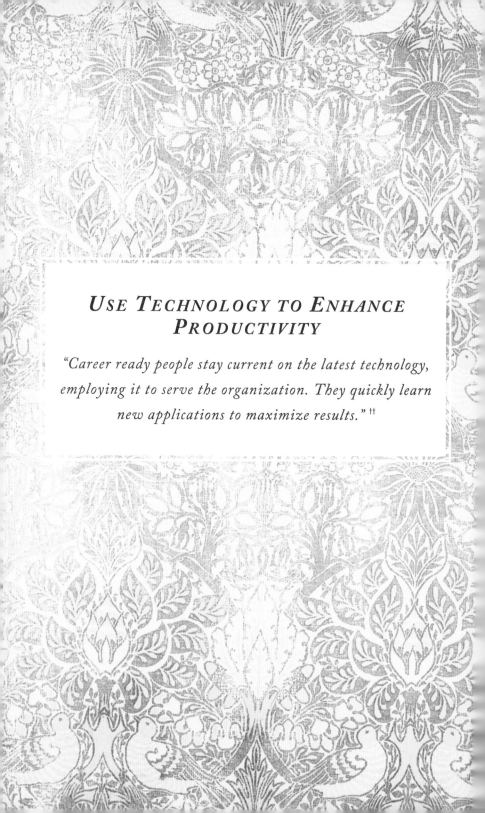

USE TECHNOLOGY TO ENHANCE PRODUCTIVITY

"Career ready people stay current on the latest technology, employing it to serve the organization. They quickly learn new applications to maximize results." [tt]

IMAGE SIX

[Immigrants and Natives]

58

IMAGE SIX
[Immigrants and Natives]

Immigrants and Natives

NATIVES ARE PEOPLE WHO RESIDE IN THEIR HOMELAND, A PLACE THAT'S FAMILIAR AND COMFORTABLE. IMMIGRANTS ARE THOSE WHO TRAVEL TO UNFAMILIAR PLACES IN ORDER TO MAKE LIFE BETTER. IN THE SAME WAY, WE MUST POSSESS THE COURAGE TO TAKE A JOURNEY TOWARD NEW TECHNOLOGY THAT'S HELPFUL AND IMPROVES OUR LIFE AND WORK.

I met Mary Martha Black when she was more than ninety years old. She still drove a car—a Toyota Prius—still did her own shopping, and regularly called me with a new idea she'd come up with that day. In short, she was still making progress, even if it was slower than when she was sixty. Instantly, I was inspired by her forward thinking.

Mary Martha is a picture of what all of us should be, no matter how old we are. She refused to be bound by old technology. She never got stuck with old methods. She was still growing mentally nine decades into her life. In the words of Stanford researcher Dr. Carol Dweck, she embraced a "growth mindset" instead of a "fixed mindset." She felt the possibilities were endless—and told me so.

What Enables People to Embrace Technology?

Ian Hosking, who works at Cambridge University's Design Centre, set out to discover why it is that as we age, we tend to get "stuck" and not embrace new technology. He saw that modern devices are designed by young people...with young people in mind. In time we eventually feel we're not on the cutting edge. So, what is it that enables people (of any age) to embrace new technology? Below are some top factors:

- *Frequency – The more people use technology, the more relaxed they are with it.*

- *Adaptability – People who are flexible and able to make adjustments tend to grow.*

- *Curiosity – Those with a hungry mind and a desire to improve usually grow.*

- *Necessity – People who need better methods to get results have incentive to learn.*

- *Optimism – If we are positive, hopeful people, we tend to embrace new things.*

ARE YOU AN IMMIGRANT OR A NATIVE?

Imagine you've entered New York Harbor as an immigrant from a foreign land. As you dock on the island, you immediately feel uncomfortable. It's not because the US is a bad place, but because it's a new place. You are very aware you're an immigrant, not a native of America. The language may be different. The customs are different. The surroundings are different. The laws are different, and the lifestyle is different. The easiest thing to do is to get back on that boat and sail right back to your home country. Ahhh…we humans love the familiar.

So it is with new technology. We often feel comfortable with what was familiar in the past. We love to feel like we've mastered that video game or that social media app; we hesitate learning something brand new. We often shy away from different and uncomfortable things. The good news is—the younger you are, the more apt you are to be a "native" of this new world. You're open to new things. The bad news is—you are growing older, and one day you will tend to get stuck like most other people do. Even though it's hard to believe, you will one day have to be very intentional about adopting new technology. Think about retired people today:

- *They grew up using phone books to find numbers. You grew up with smart phones that stored phone numbers.*

- *They grew up looking up information in encyclopedias. You grew up looking up stuff on apps on your phone or tablet.*

- *They grew up staying in touch with letters and phone calls. You grew up staying in touch with texts, Twitter, and Instagram.*

- *They grew up in the Gutenberg Era, with print on paper. You grew up in the Google Era, with digital data on a screen.*

As hard as it is to believe, though, one day—you will be the older generation.

TWO TRAITS WE NEED

What's more, it's important to remember that technology can be both constructive and destructive. It's a blessing and a curse. A knife or a scalpel in the right hands allows a doctor to perform lifesaving operations. In the wrong hands, a criminal can use it to commit murder. Like technology, a scalpel is neutral—it can help or harm.

So, we must approach technology with two goals in mind. We must be:

1. *Resourceful* – Keeping up with the best technology to help find solutions.

2. *Result-oriented* – Using it to achieve strategic goals for an organization.

These are two valuable traits to an employer. Because our world changes so rapidly, we must be resourceful, finding answers to new problems efficiently. Because our world is so noisy and cluttered, we must be result-oriented, staying focused on achieving a mission. Great team members have both traits.

To pull this off, we must ultimately be responsible with technology. This means we are perceptive as we read content online, checking what's true and what's false. This is where most students get into trouble. Dick Carlson, the Chief Learning Officer at Applied Educational Systems, said, "The most important technology skill for students is the ability to judge the quality and hidden influences of content that they encounter in the online world. Thirty years ago, most research materials available to students were vetted by some kind of gatekeepers...now students need to learn to cross-check information, check reliability of sources...and to verify what they learn."

I recently read about a student who decided to stop complaining about problems and start solving them. After studying technology, he did something amazing with it. At twenty-two years old, Tim Whitehead visited Zambia, where he heard firsthand about people dying due to lack of clean water. He became passionate about getting clean water to developing nations. Tim created a water bottle that uses a filter and a crank-powered ultraviolet light to eliminate almost all bacteria— it's a lifesaving use of creativity and technology.

Selene Chew was just twenty-three when she recognized the opportunity to do more than just master technology for school research. She invented "BlindSpot," a cane that guides blind people by using GPS. It also uses sensors to safely avoid obstacles in the path. How cool is that?

Technology can be fun and games...but when used well, it can also change the world.

THINK IT OVER, WRITE IT DOWN

1. Why do people you know often get "stuck" with old methods and technology?

_____

_____

2. Have you ever used technology to solve a "real world" problem? How?

_____

_____

3. In a job interview, would you say you're a "native" or "immigrant" to technology?

_____

_____

Evaluate Yourself

Circle the number that indicates your most accurate response:

1. How do you currently use technology in your life?

Recreation/Pleasure   1   2   3   4   5   Results/Purpose

2. Given a choice with technology, which do you tend to pursue?

Familiar/Comfortable   1   2   3   4   5   Unfamiliar/New

3. How rapidly do you adapt to new ways of doing things?

Slow Adaptor   1   2   3   4   5   Quick Adaptor

Try It Out

Get in groups of three students and research the newest technology that has been introduced into the marketplace. (It could be social media, tablets, cell phones, software, computers or some other device.) Brainstorm several ways that new technology could be used in a company to accomplish its mission. In other words, come up with ways the new device can be used for redemptive purposes, not merely entertainment purposes. Make a formal presentation in front of the class that includes images or diagrams, describing the results you could achieve with the technology in a business. Discuss the best ideas with your class.

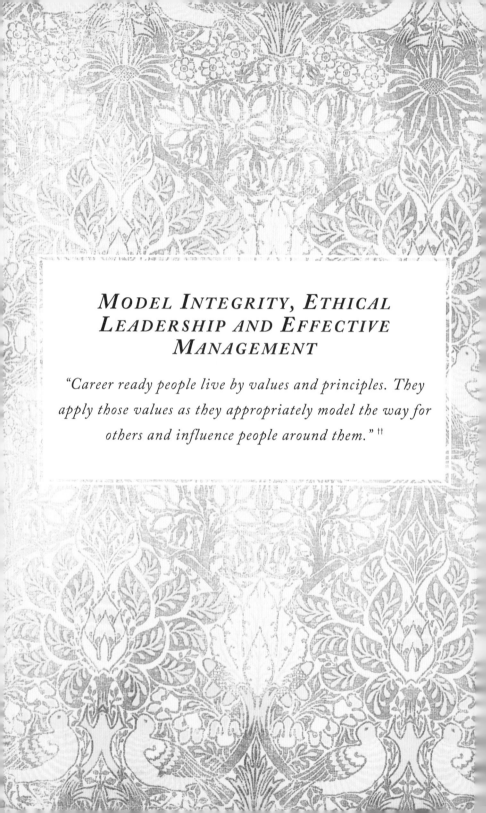

MODEL INTEGRITY, ETHICAL LEADERSHIP AND EFFECTIVE MANAGEMENT

"Career ready people live by values and principles. They apply those values as they appropriately model the way for others and influence people around them." [††]

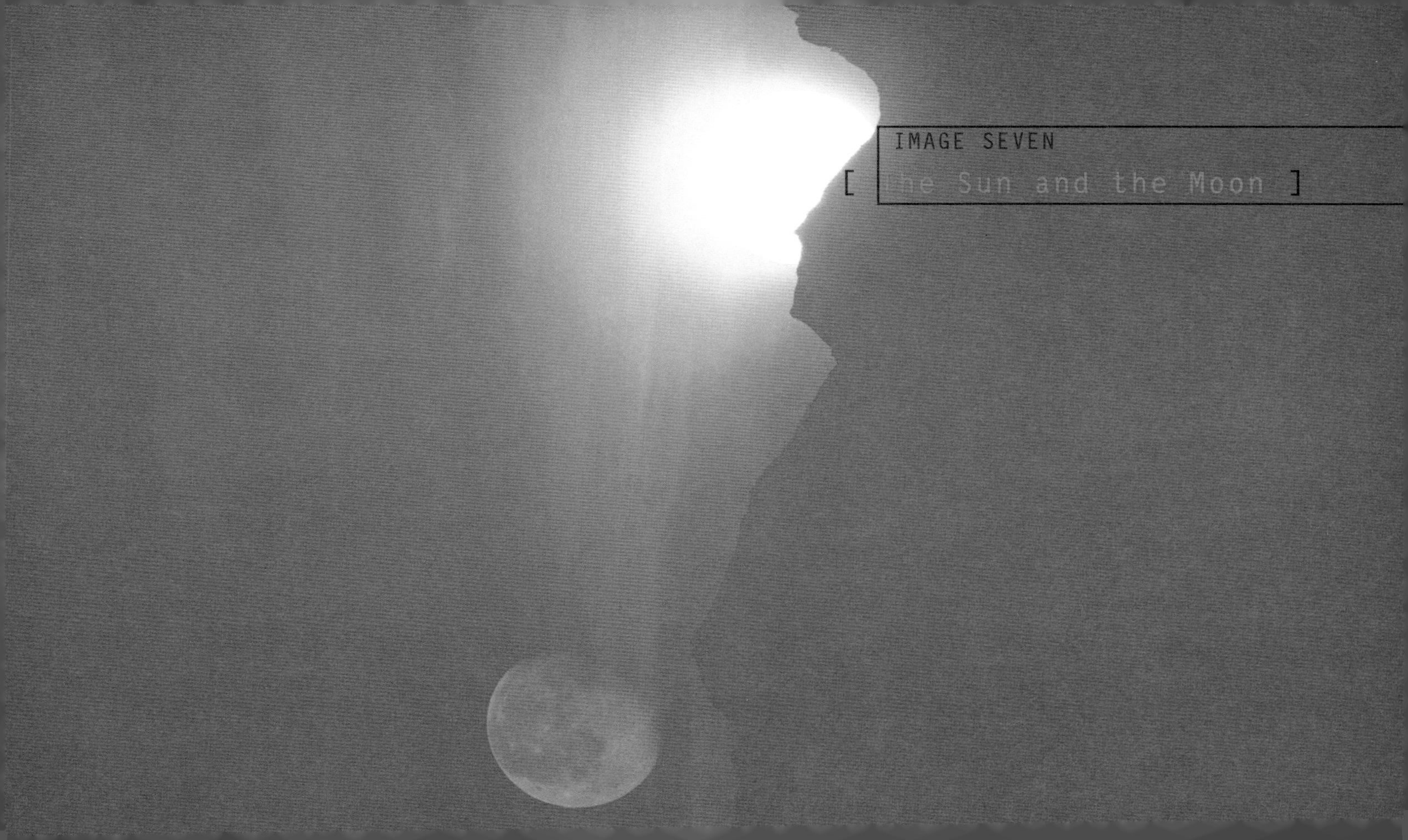

IMAGE SEVEN

[The Sun and the Moon]

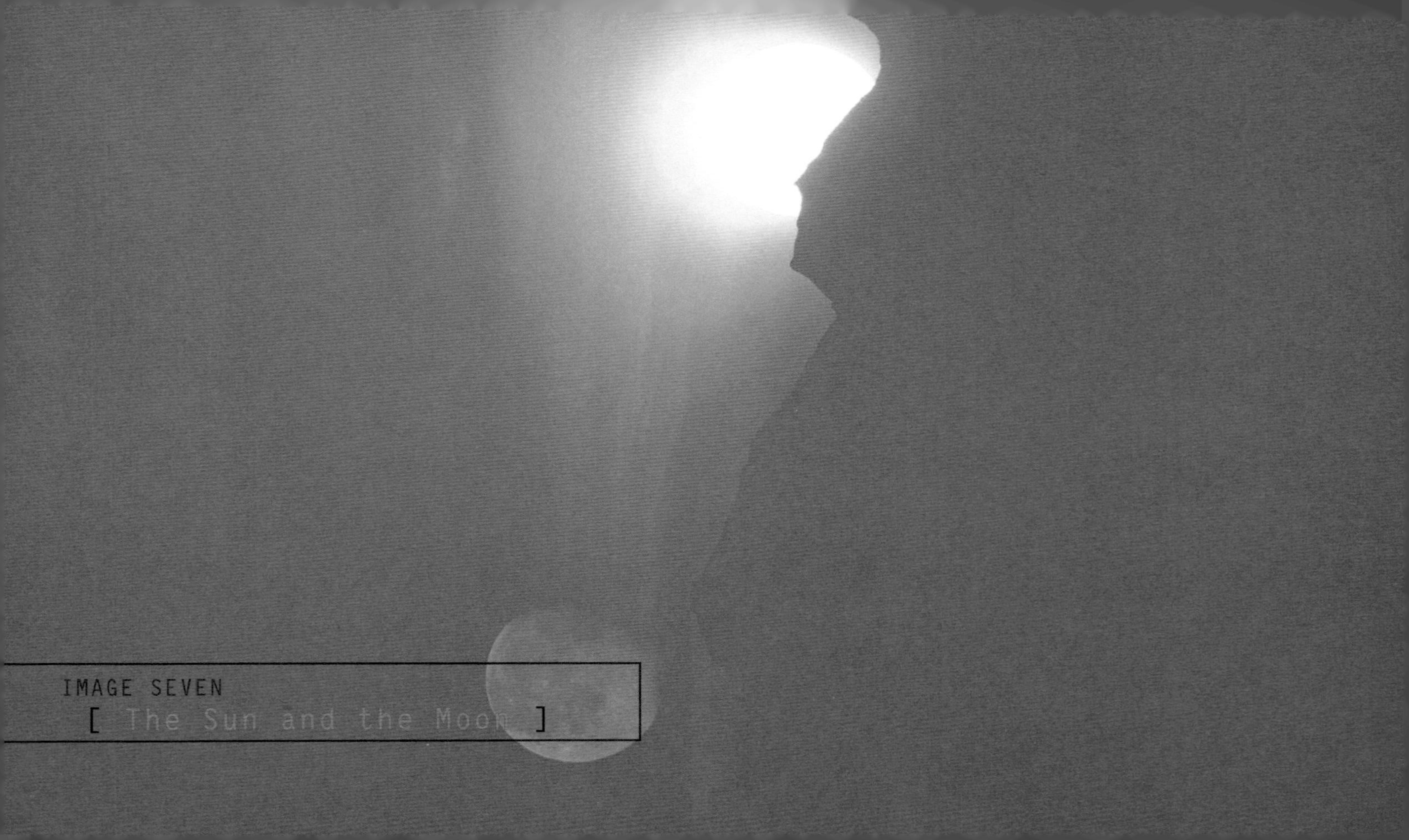

IMAGE SEVEN
[The Sun and the Moon]

The Sun and the Moon

THE SUN AND THE MOON BOTH FURNISH LIGHT FOR US. THE DIFFERENCE IS, THE MOON ONLY REFLECTS THE LIGHT THE SUN PROVIDES; THE SUN IS ACTUALLY A SOURCE OF LIGHT. IN THE SAME WAY, TO MAKE A DIFFERENCE, WE MUST GENERATE AND INITIATE; WE MUST INSPIRE OTHERS AND GO FIRST, MODELING THE WAY FOR OTHERS.

For decades now, NASA has been studying our moon, taking pictures and notes, and even landing on the moon in July 1969. I remember watching that moon landing on TV when I was a kid. It was unbelievable to see Neil Armstrong and Buzz Aldrin step off the Apollo 11 spacecraft and walk around. It seemed like a sci-fi movie.

What's even more exciting is that there are spacecrafts observing the sun right now.

The most famous spacecraft sent to observe the Sun is the Solar and Heliospheric Observatory (SOHO), built by NASA and ESA and launched in December 1995. SOHO has been continuously observing the sun since then and sending back countless images. Along the way, we've learned a ton. But I think it's easy to forget the simplest and most basic knowledge we've gained—and how it can help us understand human behavior.

I am sure you remember studying astronomy in science class. Two of the most important factors that determine our experience on earth are the sun and the moon. Think about them for a moment and compare:

- *Both the sun and the moon provide light for us.*

- *Both the sun and the moon impact our days, nights and weather.*

- *Both the sun and the moon influence us based on how close we are to them.*

I am sure you also know the big differences between the sun and the moon. They provide a picture for us about leadership and influence:

- *The sun generates light. The moon can only reflect that sunlight.*

- *The moon is rotating and revolving. The sun doesn't revolve.*

- *The sun produces elements like heat. The moon reacts accordingly.*

My goal in this chapter is not to review lunar and solar astronomy. Instead, I want to explore what we learn about relationships and leadership from the sun and the moon. I believe we can draw helpful analogies by thinking about both of their roles. While they both influence our life on earth, the fact is, while the moon is helpful, the sun is essential. The sun is the primary influence on our planet. We can't live without it.

In every organization, there are people who take after the sun and the moon. Most of the time, people emulate the moon; they are only reflections of the light someone else gives. They respond or react to others. There's nothing wrong with this, but during your career, there will be times when you'll need to step up and generate. You'll need to be the one who influences, not merely one who's being influenced by others. In some situations, you'll need to take initiative on a project, instead of waiting for someone else to do so. You'll need to ignite some passion for an idea, not just hope a colleague will do it. You will need to be a "sun" and lead the way.

The good news is, your influence is not completely dependent on your position. You don't have to be the "boss" to lead or influence others. The sun is 390 times further away from us than the moon—but it still influences. In the same way, our leadership has less to do with our position and more to do with our disposition. What are we made of? How do we relate to others? Are we trustworthy? Do we add value to people? What do we bring to the team?

Years ago, Trevor Ferrell was a middle school student who did his homework in front of the television. One night, the local news reported the story of homeless people living in his hometown of Philadelphia. The story gripped Trevor. He had no idea so many people had no house or food on cold nights. At dinner, he asked his parents if they could do something about it, and they agreed to pray for those homeless people. But that wasn't enough for Trevor. He finally convinced his mom and dad to drive downtown and pass out a meal and a blanket. His parents secretly hoped that would satisfy his appetite for such a venture. But once Trevor gave the food and blanket to someone sitting on the sidewalk, it only fueled his passion to do more. Within a year, this young teen had set up Trevor's Place, an organization that serves the homeless in Philly. By the time he graduated high school, Trevor had three hundred volunteers working to feed the poor living on the streets of Philadelphia. You might say Trevor generated sunshine for them.

How to Provide Sunshine, Not Just Moonlight

In order to be a healthy "sun," not just a "moon," consider what the sun provides:

1. *It provides light for us*
   We must shed light on issues for others, including insight, ideas and passion.

2. *It furnishes warmth for us*
   We should be warm and relational, able to empathize and connect with others.

3. *It doesn't push, it pulls*
   We should be magnetic, pulling others toward a healthy and right direction.

4. *It is stable in a rotating solar system*
   We should be consistent, living by principles, ethics and healthy values.

5. *It sustains life*
   We should be fully engaged as life-giving people in our work with teammates.

I realize you may not see yourself as a leader. You're young and inexperienced. But don't forget, you've been gifted to make a difference and positively influence people and organizations. In fact, I believe the world is full of two kinds of leaders, and everyone reading this chapter fits into one of these two kinds:

1. *Habitual Leader*
   This person leads naturally, out of habit. Whatever group or team they join, they tend to take charge. This represents ten to fifteen percent of the population.

2. *Situational Leader*
   These people don't see themselves as leaders, but when placed in the right situation, they're naturally productive, confident and influential.

Situational leaders make up eighty-five to ninety percent of the population. In other words, your best "sunlight" will arise when you find a situation that matches your identity: your gifts, your passions, your personality, your concerns, and opportunities. Your job is to find that situation where you can offer the best sunlight.

Don't make excuses like "I'm just not a natural leader" or "I'm an introvert." Social scientists tell us the most introverted of people influence 10,000 other people in an average lifetime. Whether you know it or not—you influence others. The question is, how do you influence them? There will always be situations where your proper role is to be a "moon" and reflect the example of your leaders. Yet, one of the greatest needs of our day is for people to initiate and offer "sunlight" on the path for others.

Have you ever heard of David Sarnoff?

In 1921, David was a young employee working for RCA with a big idea. The greatest boxing match of that era was about to take place between Jack Dempsey and a French fighter named Georges Carpentier. David thought it would be cool to broadcast the fight on radio. (This had never been done before). The RCA executives felt the idea was foolish. Radio, they said, was for playing classical music.

When David Sarnoff refused to give up, his boss finally allowed him to test the idea, but on his own time and money. It was all the incentive Sarnoff needed. He collected a team to help him, borrowed a military transmitter, asked a friend with a great voice to "call" the fight, and then called every RCA salesman he knew to encourage them to position radios in public places in their towns.

The rest is history. Over 300,000 people heard the fight on air, and suddenly everyone wanted a radio so they could listen to sports. By the spring of 1922, radio companies sprang up all over, and within a decade—radio transformed our lives.

At just twenty-three years old, David Sarnoff was leading the way, offering his own sunshine.

THINK IT OVER, WRITE IT DOWN

1. Why do so many people fail to see themselves as leaders?

_____

_____

2. In what situations do you feel most comfortable initiating, or being a "sun"?

_____

_____

3. In a job interview, would you say that you're a habitual or situational leader?

_____

_____

Evaluate Yourself

On a scale of one to ten, circle your honest answer as you evaluate yourself:

STATEMENT:

	Seldom									Always
I tend to jump in and go first on tasks:	1	2	3	4	5	6	7	8	9	10

	Not Really									Definitely
I like to influence other people:	1	2	3	4	5	6	7	8	9	10

	Hesitate									Initiate
When a problem arises, I often:	1	2	3	4	5	6	7	8	9	10

	Off and On									All the time
I live by my ethics and values:	1	2	3	4	5	6	7	8	9	10

Circle the term that best describes how you see yourself:

Habitual Leader   Situational Leader

Try It Out

Take time to reflect on your personal style. Jot down your response to this question:

In what situations am I most naturally a leader?

_____

_____

_____

_____

Be as thorough as possible, writing down situations and evaluating how comfortable you are stepping out and leading the way for others. Then, over the next week, place yourself in this kind of a situation and do something to set an example for others. It might be a service project, or it could be at home with your family. It's possible it could be on a sports team or a campus club. In any case, practice the principle of this chapter: play the role of the "sun," where you provide ideas and insight, good relationships, steady ethics and values and ultimately a solution to a problem. On the same page where you jotted down your situation, write out what you did and how you felt along the way. Talk it over in class. Describe your own leadership journey.

ATTEND TO PERSONAL HEALTH AND FINANCIAL WELL-BEING

"Career ready people recognize the importance of physical, mental, social and financial well-being to career success. Their personal health makes their team stronger." ††

IMAGE EIGHT

[Seeds and Fruit]

Seeds and Fruit

A FARMER UNDERSTANDS IT'S IMPOSSIBLE TO HARVEST A CROP UNLESS HE HAS FIRST PLANTED SEEDS IN HIS FIELD. SIMILARLY, WE WILL ALWAYS REAP WHAT WE SOW. WHATEVER WE PLANT IN OUR LIVES MENTALLY, EMOTIONALLY, SOCIALLY AND FINANCIALLY WILL EVENTUALLY PRODUCE FRUIT, GOOD OR BAD. CONSEQUENTLY, WE MUST INVEST WELL IN OUR FUTURE.

There's an old story of a man named Bob, who lost his car keys one night while he was downtown. Several people noticed him looking for the keys around a busy street corner. When one person approached him and asked what he was doing, he explained he was looking for his keys. When the person inquired where he last saw them, he pointed to a dark street about a block away.

The person looked at Bob and asked, "Then why aren't you looking for the keys over there where you lost them?

"It's simple," Bob replied. "The light is so much better over here."

You may have heard this ridiculous story before. It's a picture of so many people. Bob was looking for his lost keys in a place he'd never find them. He lost them on a dark street corner but preferred to hunt for them where the light was good because it's easier to see things in the light. Hmmm. It just doesn't make sense.

Very often, young people begin their careers without thinking much about the long- term impact of their decisions. They are active, doing things that won't get them where they want to go in the long run. Like Bob, they're staying where the light is good, not where they'll find what they are looking for. It is incredibly important that you remember the "Principle of the Path" as you begin your career:

It is my direction, not my intention, that determines my destination.

This simply means that my life doesn't change just because I want it to—but instead when I begin to act and move in the right direction. We don't drift into a good direction. We can't just hope for it. We must prioritize and discipline ourselves to get there.

What Are You Planting?

Consider a farmer planting crops for a moment. If he plants corn at the right time, in several months, he's going to harvest corn. He won't get wheat or apple trees. There's an old proverb that says "We reap what we sow." That farmer can only expect corn because that's what he planted. In the same way, how can we expect to receive something when we haven't planted it? Or how can we gain something for nothing? If we don't spend the time planting good habits, cultivating them, then waiting for them to emerge—we can't expect them to suddenly turn up when we're adults. It's like a bank account: you can only withdraw what you have deposited.

This chapter is all about you creating a path for a healthy life. We believe students should attend to their personal and financial well-being. No one else can do it for them. The career ready individual recognizes the importance of physical, mental, social and financial well-being to being successful in a career.

Just ask Melanie and Ben. Both of these students learned this lesson but in very different ways. Because his dad made a good salary, Ben never had to get a job during high school. Since he always had money, he never really learned how to manage it. He had a handful of friends who hung out together and played video games for hours after school. Sitting in front of a video game and eating junk food wasn't a good combination. Ben began gaining weight, which kept him from having the energy to work out at the gym. Because his friends were easy to spend time with, he didn't work to meet new people and build a network. When it was time to move out and get an apartment, he needed help from parents and friends—he wasn't ready for his career.

Now, Melanie stood as a total and complete contrast to Ben. She decided to start working out her freshman year, eating right and staying healthy all through college. Because she worked, she was able to stay out of debt and build her resume all through high school and college. In fact, she began saving money for her future.

Can you guess which one of these graduates launched quickly into a career? Ben was embarrassed. Melanie was empowered. It's a repeat of the children's story of the three little pigs. Two built houses of straw and sticks; the other built a house of bricks, and when the wolf came, it's obvious which house was able to stand.

Newton's Third Law

I am sure you remember the basic laws of physics. Newton's third law of motion is: *For every action, there is an equal and opposite reaction.*

This simply means we live in a "cause and effect" world. Actions always create results. What this means to your career is simple: what you do now will have a positive or negative effect on how your career works out later. How you manage your current life and jobs will somehow influence your life and jobs in the future.

When students fail to manage their upcoming careers well, they're not ready upon graduation. So, in 2010 Monster.com reported that sixty percent of college students moved back home when they finished college; by 2012, the number had increased to eighty percent. It's not that the students were untalented or unintelligent. They just hadn't prepared for the jobs that awaited them. The laws of physics are always in motion.

Sometimes, the failure to launch is for different reasons—like money. Financially, it's been a rocky road for recent college graduates. Between ballooning student loans, credit cards and money owed to family members, a Fidelity survey shows they're facing an average of $35,200 in college-related debt. For about half of 2013's graduates, the debt they accumulated came as a shock. About four in ten of them said if they could do it all over again, they would do things differently. It's very hard to pursue a dream when tied down with so much debt.

From Backpack to Briefcase

Let me recommend some good "seeds" to plant now that will pay off later:

1. *Create a social support system* – Build friendships with people who can offer helpful and positive emotional support as you enter your career.

2. *Stay positive and express gratitude* – The glass is half full, not half empty, if you focus on the positive elements of your life and communicate gratitude to others.

3. *Do something to improve yourself every week* – Keep growing personally; read, meet new people, find mentors, enhance your resume on a regular basis.

4. *Work to get out of debt* – Manage your finances well and avoid debt when possible Pay off credit cards on a regular basis and work to build a savings account.

5. *Always seek to add value to people* – In every interaction with people, do or say something that adds value to them; maintain a habit and attitude of service to others.

6. *Feed your mind and body well* – Read a book every month; exercise regularly to stay fit and energetic as you grow into your career.

Years ago, National Geographic ran an article about the Alaskan bull moose. The males of the species battle for dominance during the fall breeding season—literally going head to head, with antlers colliding together as they fight. Often their only weapon is their antlers, so a broken antler almost guarantees defeat.

The heftiest moose, with the largest and most durable antlers, triumphs in the end. Therefore, the battle fought in the fall is actually won during the summer, when the moose are eating continuously. The one that consumes the best diet for growing antlers and gaining weight will be the heavyweight in the fight. Those that eat inadequately have weaker antlers and less bulk. What happens in summer shows up in the fall.

So it is with us. Your healthy habits today—physically, financially, mentally and socially—will pay great dividends during your career. It's up to you to eat and exercise well and in every way. You are a product today of the decisions you made yesterday. The seeds you plant now will one day bear fruit.

THINK IT OVER, WRITE IT DOWN

1. Often, people make decisions based on the payoff today, not tomorrow. Why is it difficult to delay gratification and make choices that pay off later?

_____

_____

2. How do your current experiences illustrate the impact of your past decisions?

_____

_____

3. What "seeds" are you planting now that will improve your future career?

_____

_____

EVALUATE YOURSELF

Measure the productivity of your life today by answering these questions:

1. What have you done in the past that were "seeds" to prepare for your career?

_____

_____

2. Going forward, what outcomes do you hope to enjoy? List some career goals.

_____

_____

3. List some action steps you must take to realize those benefits.

_____

_____

Try It Out

Every positive "seed" you plant to improve your career will fall into one of two categories: your character or your competence. Decisions will either make you better on the inside or the outside. Both are important.

You must remember: your growth will likely appear less like a "microwave oven" and more like a "Crockpot." It will probably take longer than you expected. Below, list some healthy "Crockpot" decisions you must make to manage your career well:

You must also remember that building good habits works like a train moving down the railroad track. While it may feel like the track is confining to the train engineer, the track doesn't hinder; it actually helps the locomotive move swiftly onward. Below, list some healthy habits you should establish to help you progress efficiently:

Now—write down when you will take these steps. Discuss them with your class.

COMMUNICATE CLEARLY, EFFECTIVELY, AND WITH REASON

"Career ready people can express ideas well. They communicate thoughts and action plans clearly to others verbally and in print." [††]

[Tappers and Listeners]

Tappers and Listeners

IN AN EXPERIMENT ON COMMUNICATION, A GROUP OF STUDENTS WRONGLY
ASSUMED THAT THE MESSAGE THEY SIGNALED WOULD BE UNDERSTOOD.
EFFECTIVE STAFF MEMBERS KNOW THAT COMMUNICATION IS A TWO-WAY
STREET AND WORK TO ENSURE THAT MESSAGES ARE UNDERSTOOD CLEARLY IN
BOTH DIRECTIONS.

In 1990, Elizabeth Newton performed her PhD project at Stanford, called Tappers
and Listeners. Chip and Dan Heath mention it in their book Made To Stick. It
was a simple exercise where a group of individuals was divided into two teams. The
first team was called "tappers," and their job was to choose a song from a list of
twenty-five well-known songs (such as "Happy Birthday" or "The Star-Spangled
Banner") and tap out the song on a table with their fingers. The second team was
the listeners. Their job was to simply guess the song by the rhythm being tapped.
Sound simple?

In reality, the listener's job was quite difficult. Of the 120 songs that were tapped
out in Newton's experiment, only three were guessed correctly. That's 2.5 percent.
Not a very good score. Now, here's what made the experiment newsworthy. Before
they began, each tapper was asked to predict the odds of their listeners getting the
song right. The tappers predicted their odds were fifty percent. They thought they
would get their message across one time in every two. Interestingly, the tappers
only got their message across one time in forty. Why? It's simple. When tappers
tap a song out, they're hearing the song in their head. Most listeners didn't hear
the song at all, even though they heard the beat. These tappers were stunned at
how hard the listeners were working in order to guess the song. Isn't it obvious?

Unfortunately, this little exercise is repeated so many times in workplaces and
schools across our country. The one speaking has a clear message in their head,
but somewhere between their lips and their listeners' ears, the message gets lost in
translation. The one talking assumes the listeners will "get it." It's simple. The fact
is, listeners' minds are in so many different places before hearing you speak—their
biases may cause them to misunderstand the message you're sending.

It may seem hard to believe, but supervisors in the workplace say young team members are often good with portable devices but not with people; they're social but not relational.

WHAT DOES THIS HAVE TO DO WITH MY CAREER?

The truth of the matter is, communication is a huge issue for employers. They list it as the number one need in employees today—clear, complete, empathetic communication. So why is this basic need so challenging to pull off?

- *Most of us grew up in a world of screens, where messaging is different.*
- *Genuine communication requires hard work, and we can get lazy.*
- *Half of communication is listening, and many of us don't do that well.*
- *Often workplaces are filled with team members from multiple generations.*
- *We tend to assume our listener is on the same page we are on.*

George Bernard Shaw once said, "The single biggest problem in communication is the illusion that it has taken place." Quite frankly, we live in the "information age" but not the "communication age." It seems we are becoming poorer at good communication as time marches on. According to Sydney Harris, "The two words information and communication are often used interchangeably, but they signify quite different things. Information is giving out; communication is getting through."

Melanie got her first job the summer following graduation and was excited to show her supervisor her skill set. Unfortunately, she got in her own way. She brought her cell phone to orientation and kept checking incoming texts during the training. This bugged her manager. In addition, when Melanie was late getting a project done and was then criticized, she got defensive in an email. (She broke rule #1 by sending an emotionally charged message electronically.) When team members began growing distant, her supervisor met with her and asked if she had any idea why. She did not. That's when Melanie got a crash course in communication from her boss:

- *Screens are for information, not for emotion.*
- *Leave your phone at your desk when attending meetings.*
- *With two ears and one mouth, we should listen twice as much as we talk.*
- *If possible, begin discussions face-to-face before using phones or email.*

Dr. Albert Mehrabian, author of Silent Messages, conducted several studies on communication. He found that seven percent of any message is conveyed through words, thirty-eight percent through tone and attitude, and fifty-five percent through non-verbal elements such as facial expression, gestures and posture.

This means ninety-three percent of communication has nothing to do with words and can't be done well on a screen.

Authentic communication usually requires me to step into the shoes of the person I am speaking with and imagine what they will need in order to understand my message. What words will best be comprehended? What voice tone should I use? Do I need to give an example of my point? Should I ask a question? How can I listen well and earn my right to speak? What methods of communicating should I use: email, text, phone call, social media or face-to-face conversation? These are all legitimate questions if you care about getting your message across. According to psychologist Rollo May, "Communication leads to community, that is, to understanding, intimacy and mutual valuing." Even though it's work, good communication is always worth the benefits it yields. Anne Morrow Lindbergh agrees: "Good communication is as stimulating as black coffee, and just as hard to sleep after."

So what can we do?

How to Make Your Point

Years ago, Milo Frank suggested some steps that lead to great communication. He wrote a book called How to Get Your Point Across in 30 Seconds or Less. Here is a summary of his big ideas:

1. *Have an objective.*
   Know exactly what you want to say and what your goal is once you're finished.

2. *Know your listener.*
   Work to understand and empathize with your listeners.

3. *Choose the best approach.*
   Based on your objective and listener, decide how to approach the conversation.

4. *Use a "hook."*
   Choose a memorable handle or analogy for your listener to engage in and grasp.

5. *Develop the subject.*
   If your goal is big, you may have to include research or supporting information.

6. *Paint a picture.*
   People love visuals and metaphors. Ensure your message leaves a picture in them.

7. *Ask for what you want.*
   Don't settle for merely informing them. Decide what action you'd like them to take.

Sometimes it's helpful to think of our daily communication as "sonar." Signals are sent from one ship to another, but everyone must remember it involves both transmitting and receiving. It's a two-way street.

Doug Conant was hired as the new CEO of Campbell Soup Company in 2001. The organization was in serious trouble at the time, since the food industry was consolidating. Doug was brought in to turn the company around. And that's exactly what he did. The challenges he faced, however, were gigantic. At the time, the culture at Campbell Soup Company was toxic. A majority of the employees were disengaged, with no passion for their work. What's more, leaders had been hired from various companies like Pepsi, Procter & Gamble and General Mills, each bringing with them their own strategies and ideas. Compounding all of these issues, there were four generations working there. People weren't connecting. Communication was just plain bad.

So Doug started to rebuild.

He began to create a culture of good communication. He set an example of noticing the good work people did, thanking them and affirming them in front of others. He wrote ten to twenty notes by hand each day to people on staff, just to let them know he'd seen their good work. (Doug actually wrote 30,000 notes in ten years). He taught his executive leaders to view all the buzz, phone calls, emails and people stopping by not as interruptions—but as opportunities to make the company better. In short, Doug got people to connect both online and offline. What's more, he launched a cohort of promising leaders to meet with and mentor, knowing they were the future of Campbell's. He got them communicating well...which created an energized culture. Soon he had people on the same page and focusing their efforts toward the mission. This was the secret to Campbell's huge turnaround—a leader who got people connected.

Jim Rohn once said, "Take advantage of every opportunity to practice your communication skills so that when important occasions arise, you will have the gift, the style, the clarity and the emotions to affect other people."

THINK IT OVER, WRITE IT DOWN

1. Do you believe communication is vital to a team or organization? Why?

_____

_____

2. When we fail to communicate well, where does the breakdown usually occur?

_____

_____

Evaluate Yourself

Evaluate your communication below, honestly and accurately:

1. When it comes to communication, where do your strengths lie?

_____

_____

2. When it comes to communication, where do your weaknesses lie?

_____

_____

3. List two actions you could take to improve your communication skills.

_____

_____

Try It Out

Plato wrote, "Wise men talk because they have something to say; fools talk because they have to say something." Good communication isn't just about "saying something," but sharing something substantial that will add value to a listener. And if our message is valuable, it deserves our best effort.

Over the course of the next week, discipline yourself to do more communicating in person rather than through a screen. In other words, messages you would normally send through a text, Instagram, Facebook or email—make the effort to see the receiver face-to-face and talk in person. This requires work, but it is a valuable skill set.

A second exercise is even more unique. For one entire day, try staying silent. No talking at all. Practice good listening, and when you have to speak, write down your message on a piece of paper or type it on a screen. Look it over before sharing it. This will help you evaluate the weight of your words; it may lead you to throw the message away rather than share it, as you realize it isn't that important. Believe it or not, one student did this years ago for an entire year. He claimed it made him far more careful about what he said and how he said it.

When you finish either of these exercises, reflect on what you learned. Talk it over in class and determine the observations people made on communication.

UTILIZE CRITICAL THINKING TO MAKE SENSE OF PROBLEMS AND PERSEVERE IN SOLVING THEM

"Career ready people can interact with complex systems, seeing the dynamics that make them work. They can reason, assess reality, and respond intelligently." [tt]

IMAGE TEN

[3-D Glasses]

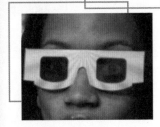

3-D Glasses

A 3-D MOVIE IS DIFFERENT THAN A TWO-DIMENSIONAL FILM. THE SPECIAL GLASSES ALLOW YOU TO EXPERIENCE HEIGHT, WIDTH AND DEPTH—ALL ANGLES OF THE STORY. SIMILARLY, VALUABLE TEAM MEMBERS SEE ALL ANGLES OF A SITUATION AND BRING CRITICAL-THINKING SKILLS WITH THEM.

When was the last time you went to a movie? How about a movie in 3-D? You know the drill. You buy your ticket—and it costs a bit more than a regular movie ticket because you have to rent special 3-D glasses. They are big and bulky, but they make the story come alive. Not long ago, I went to a 3-D movie with my family, and it was incredible…the glasses made everything pop, jump out, and appear three-dimensional. The story became even more real.

Have you ever tried watching a 3-D movie without the glasses? At this last one, I took my glasses off for a few minutes just to see what it would look like. It didn't take long for me to want to put them back on. Everything was fuzzy and distorted. I could still hear the dialogue, but the viewing was unclear. That's why they give you the glasses. If you stop and think about it, the 3-D lens:

- *Helps you perceive what's happening more clearly.*

- *Causes the plot and characters to come alive.*

- *Allows you to experience all three dimensions, not just two.*

In many ways, these 3-D glasses are a picture of what employers want in their team members. Organizations need employees who bring a special lens with them—a lens that enables them to see problems and solutions clearly; a lens that helps them perceive the root of what's really going on; a lens that ultimately allows them to carefully evaluate and know what to do. The lens aids them in seeing all three dimensions of a situation—height, width and depth. One manager told me, "I'll pay more for a staff person who can see every situation from all angles and know what to do with it. This skill helps us find solutions quicker. It's almost priceless."

A Penny for Your Thoughts

This may sound elementary to you, but you'd be surprised if you knew how many people just stop thinking once they land a job. It's like their entire goal is to simply get a job, and when they do, they turn their brain off and stop practicing critical thinking. I once read that seventy percent of Americans do no thinking of their own. Evidently, it's too much work, so they let commercials, magazines, websites, and friends do their thinking for them. Life seems so complicated that they don't trust their own judgment. They don't do any research, and they fear being wrong.

Critical thinking can be defined this way: it is the process of analyzing, evaluating and applying information as a guide to belief and action. If knowledge is possessing information, then critical thinking means knowing how to apply information wisely. In 1597, Francis Bacon was the first to say "knowledge is power." If that's true, then critical thinking means having superpowers. Knowledge becomes wisdom.

Team members who have critical-thinking skills are like people who watch movies with 3-D glasses. They see details in a more amazing way and process what others just don't see. Rich Milgram, CEO of career network Beyond, said, "The most-sought-after skill sets for recruiters are becoming less and less about proficiency in tasks and more about how you think systems through and work within the context of the team. Learning technology is the easy part. Having the mindset to apply it, having the logic to process it, being thorough and detail-oriented while doing so, these are the critical skills." Based on Milgram's research at Beyond, the top three most-sought-after skill sets were listed in nine out of ten jobs:

1. *Critical Thinking.* Using logic and reasoning to identify the strengths and weaknesses of alternative solutions, conclusions or approaches to problems.

2. *Complex Problem Solving.* Identifying complex problems and reviewing related information to evaluate options and implement solutions.

3. *Judgment and Decision Making.* Considering the costs and benefits of potential actions to choose the most appropriate ones.

So what does this look like in real life? Let me illustrate.

Critical Thinking Leads to Critical Changes

For eleven-year-old Peyton Robertson, it all began when he watched Hurricane Sandy wreak havoc across the US coastline in 2012. He was intrigued at how sandbags weren't efficient to stop the flooding. The sand couldn't prevent the water from penetrating. So what did he do? He invented a sandbag with no sand.

Peyton is from Ft. Lauderdale, Florida, so he'd seen a few storms and floods even as a kid. It's what drove him to design his new protection against floods, hurricanes and other disasters. He calls it the Sandless Operational Sandbag (SOS), and it earned him the title of "America's Top Young Scientist" in 2013. Here is his flow of thought:

- *Conventional sandbags are heavy to transport and leave gaps.*

- *We need to create a lighter sandbag that could expand to fill crevices.*

- *What if we made a bag with a combination of salt and polymer inside?*

- *The bag would be doused with water before use so the polymer expands.*

- *The mixture makes the bag light, easy to store and more effective.*

It makes sense, doesn't it? What's cool is…it works. It pays to wear 3-D glasses and see all the layers of a situation that others may not. Often people are bound by the way things have always been done. (How many years have we been using sandbags?) But Peyton's 3-D perspective helped him analyze our current methods, see that they weren't getting the job done and invent something that does.

How Do We Grow Critical Thinking Skills?

The question is far bigger than we can cover in this short chapter, but here's a start:

1. *Begin by observing your biggest problems—then ask why they exist.*

2. *Look at all angles of your reality to evaluate how it got that way.*

3. *Identify your needs: What's your goal? What does "better" look like?*

4. *Explore several solutions, then compare them to find the best one.*

5. *Evaluate what it would take to implement one—and ask "why not?"*

Critical Thinking Pays Off Big-Time

Jodie Wu was an engineering student at MIT. One of her classes challenged her to come up with a creative idea to help a developing nation. She pulled a team of students together and began collaborating with a team in Tanzania. They have redesigned bicycles to do agricultural tasks such as threshing corn in rural areas that have limited access to electricity. She and her team had to think critically to develop the idea, find ways to manufacture and distribute it, and fundraise and market the company. She is now the CEO of Global Cycle Solutions in Tanzania.

At twenty-four years old, she was named to Forbes magazine's "30 under 30" list in 2011. Because of ongoing critical thinking around the invention, the Gates Foundation backed the multi-crop thresher in 2013.

THINKING FOR YOURSELF

Way back in the 1860s, young artists like Renoir, Pissarro, Monet and Cezanne were struggling to get noticed. They were all brilliant painters but could never get their artwork on display at the famous "Palais de l'Industrie" art exhibit, where France's finest and most famous paintings were on display. Critics at the Paris Salon would judge the paintings submitted by artists and reject most of them. Since these guys had a new style—impressionism—they were among the rejects each year.

One year, however, this group of young painters asked themselves, "Do we want to continue submitting our work to the huge Salon and perhaps get rejected forever? And, even if accepted, merely be one of thousands of paintings? Or do we strike out on our own and stage a show for our own genre—impressionism." They met and did some critical thinking. They discussed and evaluated the situation...and in the end, chose to launch their own show. I am so glad they did. It's the reason their work is now hanging in every great museum around the world today. These artists are now famous—because of two reasons: a new style...and some fabulous critical thinking.

The fact is—those young artists saw something others couldn't see. They perceived where culture was heading, and instead of fitting in, they stood out, choosing a new style and creating their own art exhibit, instead of mimicking the current one.

THINK IT OVER, WRITE IT DOWN

1. Why do you think most people don't do a lot of deep thinking?

_____

_____

2. In what area do you find yourself doing your best critical thinking?

_____

_____

3. Where are you able to see a wide variety of perspectives and options?

_____

_____

Evaluate Yourself

Evaluate your thought processes below, as accurately as possible, scoring yourself on a scale of one to ten (ten being the highest level of agreement):

I analyze situations around me well: 1 2 3 4 5 6 7 8 9 10

I can see many angles and perspectives: 1 2 3 4 5 6 7 8 9 10

I can scrap my ideas if they don't work best: 1 2 3 4 5 6 7 8 9 10

I think deeply about problems to solve them: 1 2 3 4 5 6 7 8 9 10

I make good decisions after careful thought: 1 2 3 4 5 6 7 8 9 10

Try It Out

With a team of classmates, watch a news program on television this week. From the broadcast, choose one report containing a dilemma or crisis, and imagine you are in charge of thinking through the best solution. In other words, select a current news report that requires critical thinking and decision-making and—in a team of three—map out the problem, the possible solutions, and what course of action you would take if you were assigned to solve the problem. Afterward, report to your class, informing them of the thought process you went through to arrive at your conclusion. Discuss it with your entire class.

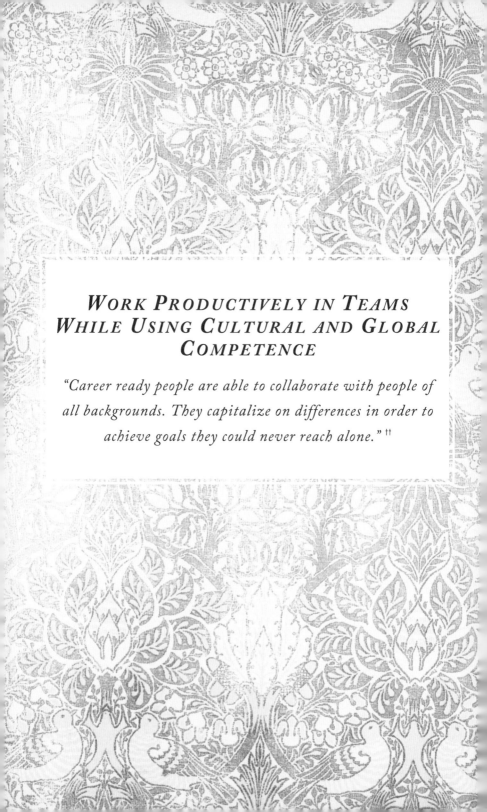

WORK PRODUCTIVELY IN TEAMS WHILE USING CULTURAL AND GLOBAL COMPETENCE

"Career ready people are able to collaborate with people of all backgrounds. They capitalize on differences in order to achieve goals they could never reach alone." [††]

[Soloists and Symphonies]

Soloists and Symphonies

CONCERTS ARE EITHER SOLOS OR SYMPHONIES—THEY'RE PERFORMED BY A SINGLE INDIVIDUAL OR A GROUP OF MUSICIANS. WHEN MORE THAN ONE PERSON PERFORMS, MUSICIANS PLAY DIFFERENT ROLES, HARMONIZING WITH THE MELODY. THE MUSIC GETS RICHER AS PEOPLE ASSUME DIFFERING ROLES YET WORK TO COOPERATE RATHER THAN COLLIDE. SO IT IS WITH TEAMS IN THE WORKPLACE.

My uncle has played the cello his entire life. He's now a professional cellist in Boise, Idaho. Over the years, he has played solo, in small ensembles, and in symphonies made up of dozens of brilliant musicians. To this day, I still enjoy watching and listening to him perform in concert.

Years ago, we talked about the difference between playing a solo concert and playing in a symphony. He said something in passing that I've thought about over and over since: Playing alone is a tradeoff. It is much easier because you only have to be mindful of yourself; yet at the same time it's harder, because all the pressure to be memorable is on you. On the other hand, playing in an ensemble (even a small one) or a symphony is more difficult because there are other people to work around, yet it is liberating to share the responsibility of the performance. Audiences recognize the paramount effort that goes into preparing for such a concert, and the coordination of so much talent. They can hear the richness of the melody and sense the beautiful harmony the instruments create. In the end, you're more likely to get a standing ovation for a symphony concert than a solo one.

I believe we can learn something from this reality. As you enter your career, you'll immediately see the need to work alongside others. Playing or working on a team means slowing down and making sure everyone's on board with the goal and collaborating with each other. At times, you might feel it would be easier to "do it by yourself." There's definitely a tradeoff when you're forced to cooperate with a bunch of other people. Yet—the tradeoff is almost always worth it. To experience a team of very different people with a variety of talents work "in concert" with each other to pull off a huge goal is unforgettable. Most of the time, teams can achieve objectives that individuals cannot.

John Maxwell used to say, "One is too small of a number to do anything extraordinary."

The Value of "Us"

All of this requires us to work at relationships—especially relationships with people who are different than we are. Sometimes they will be cross-cultural relationships, where you'll have to work extra hard at understanding a different background, language, customs and values. Yet it's amazing how fulfilling it can be to join hands and work together to pull off something neither of you could do alone.

One of my favorite bands is U2. Lead singer Bono is known all over the world, and he and his band have filled stadiums for over thirty years now. But do you know they don't see themselves as simply a rock band? They are a team of very different artists with different skill sets, yet with a single mission.

When they launched in the 1970s, all four band members agreed upon their values and vision—that they would be about social justice, not just songs. In other words, their music had a mission: to promote human rights and to end poverty. Once they signed their agent, they agreed the five of them would make decisions together and never move forward on big ones until they all agreed. They would act as brothers, and if one was experiencing personal trouble, they would all have his back and support him. They would also split the money evenly five ways.

During the 1980s this spirit of teamwork became vividly clear. They were touring the US and singing one of their hit songs, "Pride (In the Name of Love)." The song is about Dr. Martin Luther King Jr., and U2 was promoting the idea of creating a holiday in his honor. When they arrived at some cities, however, they got mixed reviews. Some did not like what the song stood for. In fact, in one city Bono received a death threat—saying he would be shot and killed onstage if he sang it.

As U2 discussed the issue, everyone except Bono believed they should drop the song from their playlist. It wasn't worth getting shot at onstage. But Bono refused to give in. After all, this message was what they stood for. He finally won the argument, knowing he'd be a sitting duck as he sang that night. Bono said later that when he began singing it he closed his eyes, just waiting for bullets to fly. When he opened them, however, he looked up to see that his fellow band members were taking turns stepping in front of him to guard him and take the bullet.

Different Is Good

This principle is not merely valuing we more than me. It's about recognizing that often our differences can be the very ingredients that make us valuable. According to a study done by Dr. Rebecca Bigler at the University of Texas, people tend to migrate toward others who are like them—as early as preschool age—and it may have nothing to do with ethnic background. Bigler's findings show that kids are developmentally prone to in-group favoritism; children categorize everything from people to food to toys at a young age. Further, Bigler contends that once a child identifies someone as most closely resembling himself, the child likes that person the most. The bottom line?

- *We naturally tend to hang around people who are similar.*

- *We are prone to like those who are like us.*

- *We tend to prejudge those who are not like us.*

- *We tend to shy away from those who are different.*

Sadly, when we do this, we miss amazing opportunities, and we move in the opposite direction of where most workplaces are going:

- White males occupied five percent fewer management jobs in 2006 than in 1998, and every other racial/gender group occupied more management jobs.

- The US population of foreign-born residents is 12.4 percent, an amount of international diversity that the US has not seen since 1920.

- Ninety percent of leading executives from sixty-eight countries named cross-cultural leadership as the top management challenge of the next century. ,

- The proportion of revenue coming from overseas markets is expected to jump by an average of thirty to fifty percent over the next three to five years.

What Are the Advantages of Diversified Teams?

Consider the benefits of collaborating with people who are different than you:

1. It helps prevent "groupthink," where everyone has the same perspective.

2. It forces you to think, act and engage in relating to team members.

3. It enables teams to think creatively, fostering "out of the box" solutions.

4. It encourages team members to focus on what each person is good at doing.

5. It accelerates productivity, as you can better reach diverse customers.

6. It discourages the comparison trap and helps people appreciate each other.

GETTING OUT OF OUR LITTLE BOX

If we're going to do this well, we must see beyond our personal interests. My vision must be bigger than gaining what benefits me, getting noticed, or hanging out with who's most comfortable for me. Life isn't about finding others who are similar, but different, and then using that difference to positively influence your world. In other words, how can we take brass, strings, woodwinds and percussion and make a symphony? Symphonies don't need every musician to play strings—they need variety. When I do this, I stop worrying about being the "star." The music and rewards are far better.

The Boston Red Sox are a prime example. In 2012, they finished in last place in their division. This baseball team had a history of disappointing fans, once going eighty-six years without winning the World Series. 2012 was just another disappointing season.

But 2013 would be different. They put together an incredibly diverse team, with players from many different countries, including Mexico, Japan, Aruba, Venezuela, Canada, the Dominican Republic and Puerto Rico and the US. The team looked a bit like the United Nations. Each of them brought unique value to the team. They spoke different languages; players were both old and young; they had different skin colors and a variety of customs. But boy—did they play well together. In 2013, they went from worst to first, winning their third World Series title since 2004. You might even say it was their diversity that enabled them to win. They knew they had to work to connect with each other, to perform in sync and to communicate well. This work drove them to play to each other's strengths. Different is beautiful. The truth is, when you begin with diversity, not uniformity, it usually pays off in the end.

THINK IT OVER, WRITE IT DOWN

1. Why is it so many people are into themselves and their own self-expansion?

_____

_____

2. How does this ego sabotage us and keep us from valuing differences in other people?

_____

_____

3. Why do people tend to want and expect others to be like them?

_____

_____

4. When have you experienced the value of very different people on a team?

_____

_____

EVALUATE YOURSELF

On the scale below, circle your most honest and accurate responses:

I work to see the value of others who are different from me.

Never   1   2   3   4   5   6   7   8   9   10   Always

I seek out others who have strengths where I'm weak, to learn from them.

Never   1   2   3   4   5   6   7   8   9   10   Always

I value other team members and prefer to work in cooperation, not alone.

Never   1   2   3   4   5   6   7   8   9   10   Always

TRY IT OUT

This week, set a goal to accomplish something you could not possibly do alone. In fact, choose a project that requires people with different talents and perspectives than you possess yourself. Make sure it is big and challenging. It could be something on your school campus, at work, or in your community.

Next, list the steps required to achieve this goal. Make a plan, listing the necessary steps along the way to get the job done. Then choose the appropriate people who have strengths that complement your own, and invite them to help you with the project. Communicate the goal and the deadline clearly, and set times to meet to discuss how you will collaborate on the project. Lead the way, and see it through to the end. Celebrate, then take time to reflect on the work you've pulled off.

Discuss your experience with your class. What did you learn?

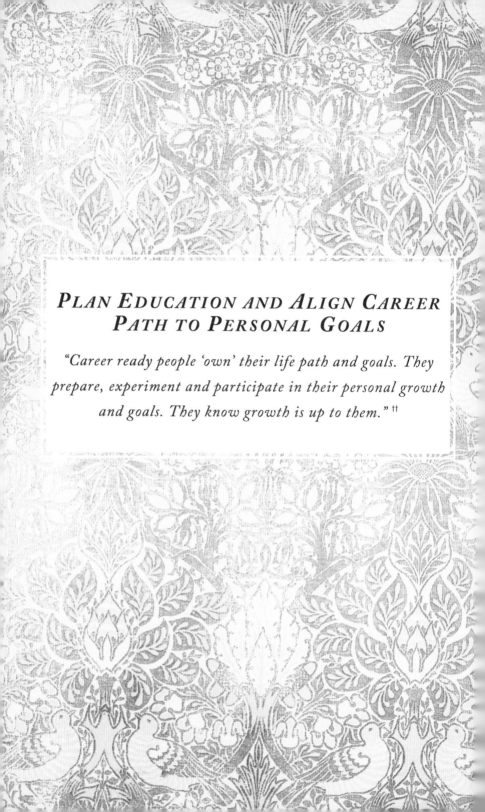

PLAN EDUCATION AND ALIGN CAREER PATH TO PERSONAL GOALS

"Career ready people 'own' their life path and goals. They prepare, experiment and participate in their personal growth and goals. They know growth is up to them." [tt]

IMAGE TWELVE
[Brands and Labels]

Brands and Labels

PEOPLE MAKE PURCHASES BASED ON BRANDS THEY CAN TRUST. EVERY BRAND HAS A LABEL, INDICATING THE QUALITY OF THE PRODUCT TO CUSTOMERS. IN THE SAME WAY, EVERY EMPLOYEE HAS A BRAND, WHETHER THEY KNOW IT OR NOT. SUCCESSFUL PEOPLE MANAGE THEIR CAREER BY BUILDING A STRONG PERSONAL BRAND AND LABEL.

Have you ever noticed how powerful a product's brand is? What comes to mind when you hear the brand name…

- *Twitter?*

- *Apple?*

- *Abercrombie & Fitch?*

- *Facebook?*

Every year, legal battles ignite between companies who claim to own the rights to a name, a logo, a formula, an image or some intellectual property. Even though nothing stops either company from creating a product similar to the original, each wants to own the "brand" that started it all. In 2013, big-name drug makers battled generic drug makers who'd sold "copycats" of their medications. After spending lots of time and money on building their "brand," the big companies didn't want to lose that investment to some generic brand. So they spent millions more dollars to protect it.

Brands are important because they carry all kinds of credibility and influence. Sometimes a brand can be so huge, people ask for it by name. When people want a soft drink at a restaurant, they'll often say, "I want a Coke." When people want a tissue, they ask for a Kleenex. When they want a bandage for their finger, they ask for a Band-Aid. These companies have become synonymous with the product they make. Their brand owns the market.

Farmers who own livestock understand the importance of a brand. People have branding cattle for thousands of years. They brand them so as to identify who cattle belongs to, and sometimes even their place of origin. The brand is actually a mark on the cow that leaves no doubt about their owner or pedigree.

People have brands too. In December 2013, Nelson Mandela, the former president of South Africa, passed away. Two weeks later, the fight was on for his brand. Family members fought with the African National Congress and his foundation for rights to his name and the phrase Long Live Mandela. Why? Because it carried such clout. Rival politicians battled over ownership of his legacy in the next general election. What's more, an intense conflict surfaced over the iconic Mandela brand as family members began to sell products using the Mandela name. They all knew his popularity would make selling easy because of what he stood for.

Whether you know it or not, you are building your own brand as well. Right now. You have a reputation; you have a style of your own; you have a personality, experiences, talents and passions—all kinds of assets to offer to a future employer. Whether you know it or not, you communicate your brand on Instagram, in your Facebook profile, through texts and emails you send, and even through the clothes you wear. These things are like labels. In the same way a tag on your clothing identifies its brand, all your actions and words are the ways people see and hear you—and come to think of you. Labels usually communicate the logo and image of the product, while the brand is all about the reputation. If your brand isn't good, it doesn't matter how nice your label looks.

The key is to be aware of it and to build your brand on purpose. For instance, if you had a job interview and then your potential employer decided to visit your Facebook page, what would they find? Would something cause them to avoid you and move on to the next candidate?

Jennifer was all about image in high school. Her clothes, her jewelry, her daily photos on Instagram—all created an image of being sassy, a maverick, someone who always got what she wanted. She had no idea she was building a reputation for being self-absorbed; people saw her as untrustworthy and unpredictable. She thought she was being whimsical, but others actually viewed her as volatile and moody. What's more, Jennifer was trying to be somebody she wasn't. She hung around a group of popular girls—and she became fake. She was forcing friendships in order to look a certain way and fit a certain style. Upon graduation—she had no prospects. She had not prepared for the working world, and she never got close to the people who could help her do so. In fact, employers avoided her after seeing what she posted online and hearing people talk about her. In short, Jennifer neglected to think about the impact of the brand she was building or the labels she was wearing. She learned you can't just make up a brand—you must be true to yourself and play to your strengths. When you do, your brand and labels match. If you fail to, your brand is artificial.

Owning an Identity

I have noticed that successful companies that build their brand intentionally are very good at "owning" a word or a phrase in the minds of their customers. They've boiled down what they do to a single idea. For instance, when most people think of:

- *Volvo…they think of "automobile safety."*

- *FedEx…they think "overnight."*

- *Crest toothpaste…they think "it fights cavities."*

- *BMW…they think of "quality."*

So, here's my question: As you launch your career, what will your brand be? What word or phrase will you own? What will be the big idea you want people to think of when they think of you? What will define your identity and vision? Some of the best-selling products on the market "own" an identity. It's more than just a look. It's about what the product can do; it's about performance, not appearance.

It works a little like a toolbox. You carry an imaginary toolbox with you each day. You are filling it with knowledge, experiences, skills and relationships that will make you more valuable or less valuable to the marketplace. You are either preparing for the future or you are just surviving, living from day to day. Your toolbox is either filling up or remaining empty. When you fail to get ready for tomorrow, you end up with much more work to compensate for later. My warning is this: if you are not preparing today, you will be repairing tomorrow.

As you can imagine, building a brand doesn't happen overnight. It took Coca-Cola decades to become the number one brand in the world—and they are still managing their name. Similarly, managing your career takes a lifetime. It requires:

- *Choosing a career path based on your strengths and interests.*

- *Seeing each job and task as an opportunity to grow.*

- *Keeping the big picture in mind as you progress through your career.*

It's Your Story

It's up to you to manage your career. Most do not have the luxury of having someone else do it for them, like an agent or a personal assistant. Your life is like a fingerprint. It is a one-of-a-kind mixture of qualities that you can offer to an organization. Your brand is like a property or a patent that you own. It's important to work so you can be proud of who you are and what you offer; yet, it's not just about building your personal fame. It's about becoming valuable to others. Albert Einstein said it best: "Don't seek to be a person of importance. Seek to be a person of value."

I met Barrett Jones when he was a junior at the University of Alabama. He played football for coach Nick Saban and the national champion Crimson Tide. His story is far bigger than football, however. Barrett played three positions during his time in college—and was an All-American at all three. He graduated in five years with both a bachelor's and master's degree, keeping a 4.0 GPA. He led service projects overseas in developing nations. When a horrible tornado swept through Tuscaloosa in 2011, Barrett spent his one day off going door to door, offering to chop the trees that had fallen on victims' homes. Coach Saban said Barrett was not only a joy to coach, but was one of the top five most influential people in his life. Not bad for a twenty-three-year-old. When he graduated, Barrett had many job offers because he had built such a strong work ethic and had so much experience. He decided to enter the NFL and was immediately picked up in the draft. I think I know why. Barrett is not just a good athlete, he's a complete human being who built a great brand while in school.

His brand and label can still be felt on the Alabama campus.

THINK IT OVER, WRITE IT DOWN

1. Why do so many people end up building a negative "brand" for themselves?

_____

_____

2. If building a personal brand is about more than choosing a style, but about discovering who you really are—how should a person go about this discovery?

_____

_____

3. What are you doing to build your personal brand and label?

_____

_____

Evaluate Yourself

Place a mark along the dotted line to indicate an honest and accurate response:

1. I am very intentional about building my network, resume and work experience.

YES ---NO

2. I am conscious of how my decisions today affect my future jobs and career.

YES ---NO

3. I am consistently thinking about how my actions will prepare me for my career.

YES ---NO

Try It Out

Take time to reflect on your personal brand. On a computer or a pad of paper, write out the words that describe the "brand" you hope to build as you enter your career. Think about your reputation. Consider your talents. Reflect on your desires and passions inside. As you list your descriptive words, leave room under each one to jot down how to build a brand around it. Limit your list to six to eight words.

For each word, list your response to the following:

- *Who could you interview who embodies this characteristic?*
- *What job experience could you gain to enable you to practice it?*
- *What books can you read to deepen your understanding of it?*
- *What service project would provide a good opportunity to model it?*
- *What leaders should you ask to equip you to make it a lifestyle?*

Discuss your personal brand and label with your class. What makes you unique?

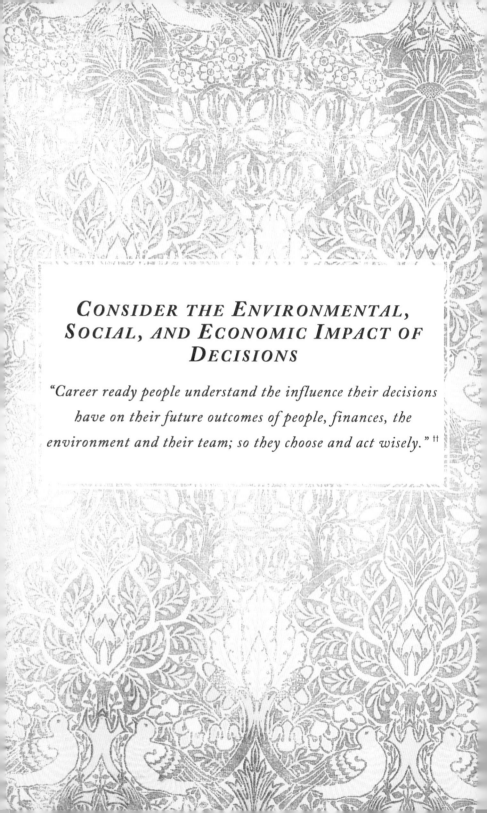

CONSIDER THE ENVIRONMENTAL, SOCIAL, AND ECONOMIC IMPACT OF DECISIONS

"Career ready people understand the influence their decisions have on their future outcomes of people, finances, the environment and their team; so they choose and act wisely." [††]

IMAGE THIRTEEN

[Butterfly Effect]

Butterfly Effect

THE FLAPPING WINGS OF A BUTTERFLY, HOWEVER SMALL, ACTUALLY AFFECT WEATHER CONDITIONS AND CONSEQUENTLY THE COURSE OF OUR LIVES. IT'S A SCIENTIFIC LAW THAT THE TINIEST OF ACTIONS CAN IMPACT FUTURE RESULTS. EVERY ACTION HAS AN EQUAL AND OPPOSITE REACTION. SUCCESSFUL TEAM MEMBERS LEVERAGE THIS AS THEY CHOOSE THEIR ACTIONS AND ATTITUDES.

My guess is, you've probably watched the classic film, "Back to the Future." It was the top grossing movie of 1985. It's the amazing story of a seventeen-year-old boy, Marty, who is accidentally sent back in time from 1985 to 1955 in a time-travel machine. It was built from a DeLorean by eccentric scientist, Emmett Brown. Marty soon learns that time-travel is more complicated than he suspected. Soon after his arrival in 1955, Marty's mother falls in love with him rather than with his father, George—threatening to cause a paradox that would result in Marty's non-existence.

The problem is further complicated when Biff Tannen, George's bully and future supervisor, pursues Lorraine (who was supposed to be George's wife and Marty's mom). Marty must find the 1955 Doc Brown to help him reunite George and Lorraine and return to 1985. In the end, Marty successfully causes his parents to fall in love and convinces his dad to finally stand up to Biff. Returning to the future, Marty discovers a vastly improved world for his family, as Biff is an auto detailer rather than George's boss. Marty's involvement, while seemingly insignificant, changed everything.

The movie is all about how small actions can completely change the trajectory of history—sending people's lives down different paths. In short, it's a vivid illustration of the "Butterfly Effect."

The Scientific Theory

In 1963, Edward Lorenz offered this hypothesis to the New York Academy of Science: A butterfly could flap his wings and set molecules of air in motion, which would move other molecules of air, and in turn, move other molecules of air, eventually capable of starting a hurricane on the other side of our world. Lorenz called the theory, "The Butterfly Effect."[xix]

It seemed far fetched and many chuckled at this preposterous theory. Yet, everyone was fascinated by it. Over time, the so-called "Butterfly Effect" became a standard for science fiction, believed to lie somewhere between myth and legend.

Thirty years later, however, the theory was proven to be credible.

Imagine the scientific community's shock when physics professors from universities across the globe came to the conclusion that this theory was accurate and credible. Soon, it was called a "law" of nature. It is now known as The Law of Sensitive Dependence Upon Initial Conditions. Further, this reality has proven to encompass more than mere butterfly wings and weather. The Butterfly Effect can be seen everywhere you go…the first movement of any kind influences our life. Edward Lorenz proved that the tiniest of actions can impact future results.

Joshua Chamberlain Did It!

Case in point. Author Andy Andrews suggests that a 34-year-old school teacher from Maine completely changed the course of American history during the Civil War.

Joshua Chamberlain signed up to help the Union army and soon became a Colonel. On July 2, 1863, he was in the fight of his life. The Battle of Gettysburg was heated and the Confederates had wiped out most of the Union army. Josh Chamberlain's troops had dwindled from 1,000 soldiers to 80. Somehow his regiment had held off four attacks by the Rebels, before they faced a fifth and final attack. Chamberlain had been hit by a bullet, and his soldiers had run completely out of ammunition. The "Lookout Boy" up in a tree yelled that the Rebels had added reinforcements and were marching forward to attack again. One of Chamberlain's officers asked which way he planned to retreat. It was a rational question.

Chamberlain later wrote about that day in his journal: "I felt sorry for my men. Their leader had no real knowledge of warfare or tactics. I was only a stubborn man and that was my great advantage in this fight. I had, deep within me, the inability to do nothing. I knew I may die, but I also knew I would not die with a bullet in my back. I would not die in retreat."

In response to his officer, Chamberlain said they would not retreat. Then—he made the most illogical decision. He gave a ridiculous order: "Fix bayonets . . . and charge! Charge! Charge!"

Chamberlain mounted the wall they hid behind and led the charge. Then . . . magic happened. When the confederates saw the 80 Union soldiers charging, screaming at the top of their lungs, they assumed these guys must be reinforcements. The rebels stopped dead in their tracks. Many dropped their weapons and ran. In less than ten minutes, Chamberlain and his 80 men had captured all 400 hundred Confederates. The tiny unit with no ammunition overtook the larger, fully-loaded enemy—and won.

Most Americans don't know this story, much less how the Butterfly Effect plays out:

- Historians believe if Chamberlain had not charged that day, the rebels would have won Gettysburg and within weeks, the Civil War.

- Those same historians believe the result would have been not merely a divided USA, but a land split between nine and thirteen countries.

- This means, when Hitler swept across Europe, there would be no USA to stand in opposition to stop the Nazis.

- It also means when Hirohito invaded the South Pacific islands, there would have been no country strong or wealthy or big enough to stop him.

Joshua Lawrence Chamberlain is a powerful example of the Butterfly Effect. One decision that day in Gettysburg changed the trajectory of history.

WHAT DOES THIS HAVE TO DO WITH ME?

While this idea is interesting, you might be asking—what does this have to do with my work and career? In one word: everything.

Wise team members recognize how the Butterfly Effect should guide decisions they make during work hours—and even after hours. Everything you do and say matters. This law can work for you . . . or against you. Consider the stories of those who failed to see this law's impact:

- Trever posted pictures on Facebook and Instagram of his amazing party last week, forgetting his Monday job interview. His potential employer saw them and dismissed him, not wanting to take a chance on this "party boy." Oops.

- Haley didn't like Jessica, her work colleague. She tried to sabotage Jessica's assignment—not realizing how it affected her own project. In the end, everyone found out and Haley was fired. She was seen as a liability.

- Justin started working for a new company—but didn't want to do more than the bare minimum to get his paycheck. When it came time for promotions, he was never considered. Promotions went to those who exceeded expectations.

- Sara kept her nose clean at work, but gossiped about her teammates at the bar on Friday nights. While listeners laughed with her, eventually, her gossip came back to bite her. Word always got back to her team and supervisor.

Every Movement Compounds—Positive or Negative

The bottom line is—we never act in a vacuum. What we say and do always causes some reaction. Any initial force leads to another force. An initial word leads to other words. So my question is: what are your words and actions generating?

When you make a decision, do you consider factors such as the environment? How about the economy? How about your affect on other people?

According to the National Technical and Career Ready Standards: "Career-ready individuals understand the interrelated nature of their actions and regularly make decisions that positively impact or reduce the negative impact on other people, organizations and the environment. They are aware of and utilize new technologies, understandings, procedures, materials and regulations affecting the nature of their work as it relates to the impact on the social condition, the environment and profitability of the organization."

Everything you say and do matters. Big or small. Negative or positive. On the job or after hours. Like it or not, you influence history.

There's a legend of an old man who walked across a beach, full of starfish that had been swept up on the shore by the tide. One by one, the man picked up the starfish, admired their beauty, then tossed them back into the water so they could live.

Along the way, someone saw the elderly man, and asked, "What are you doing?"

The old man just smiled and said, "I am saving the starfish."

"Are you kidding?" was the reply. "Just look at the beach—there are hundreds of them. You'll never be able to save them all. What difference does it make?

In that moment, the old man had just thrown a starfish into the water. As he did, he simply responded, "It made a difference to that one."

Think It Over, Write It Down

1. Most people don't consider the ripple effect of their decisions. They're only focused on their own lives. Why is this?

_____

_____

2. Can you name a time when you saw someone say or do something that had a surprising amount of influence on a situation?

_____

_____

3. Do you have a decision in front of you that could have a big-time Butterfly Effect?

_____

_____

Evaluate Yourself

Circle the most honest and accurate response to the question below:

When I make a decision about what I say or do, usually I am thinking about…

- How it will benefit me
- The here and now
- Making the easiest choice
- How it will appear to others
- A narrow focus or perspective

- How it will impact others
- The long-term future
- Making the wisest choice
- What it will actually produce
- The big picture

Try It Out

Write down one big decision you are facing right now. It could be about a personal, school, job or extra-curricular activity.

Big decision: _____

_____

Now, list how your decision will influence:

Your family: _____

_____

Your siblings : _____

_____

Your grades: _____

_____

Your money: _____

_____

The environment: _____

_____

Your time: _____

_____

The future: _____

_____

Your reputation: _____

_____

After considering these categories, did it help you make a better decision?

_____

_____

_____

Afterward, talk about building a habit of seeing the long-term effect of your choices.

[End Notes]

i   NPR Staff and Wires, "Elizabeth Edwards: Resilience Remembered." NPR, December 8, 2010.

ii   Gary Wolf, "Steve Jobs: The Next Insanely Great Thing." Wired, April 2002.

iii "Best Young Inventors and Their Inventions." MSN, October 17, 2011.

iv Andy Stanley, The Principle of the Path. Thomas Nelson, 2011.

v   Blake Ellis, "Class of 2013 Grads Average $35,200 in Total Debt." CNN Money, May 17, 2013.

vi Chip Heath and Dan Heath, Made to Stick: Why Some Ideas Survive and Others Die. Random House, 2007. 19-20.

vii Marcel Robles, "Executive Perceptions of the Top Ten Soft Skills Needed in Today's Workplace." Business Communication Quarterly, 2012.

viii Dina Gerdeman, "Pulling Campbell's Out of the Soup." Harvard Business School, March 22, 2013. http://hbswk.hbs.edu/item/7133.html

ix Meghan Casserly, "The 10 Skills That Will Get You Hired In 2013." Forbes, December 10, 2012.

x   Echoing Green, "Jodie Wu." 2010 Echoing Green Fellows. www.echoinggreen.org/fellows/jodie-wu

xi Matthew Harper, "Rising Stars of Science: The Forbes 30 Under 30." Forbes, December 19, 2011.

xii Press Release, Grand Challenges Explorations. May 21, 2013. http://www.grandchallenges.org/about/Newsroom/Pages GCERound10Grants.aspx

xiii Po Bronson and Ashley Merryman, NurtureShock: New Thinking About Children. Twelve, 2009. Chapter 1.

xiv Ruth Ellen Wasem, "Immigration Reform: Brief Synthesis of Issue." CRS Report For Congress, August 23, 2007. Available at http://fpc.state.gov documents/organization/91856.pdf

xv Equal Employment Opportunity Commission's raw data.

xvi Economist Intelligence Unit, "CEO Briefing: Corporate Priorities for 2006 and Beyond." The Economist Intelligence Unit. http://graphics.eiu.com/files/ad_pdfs ceo_Briefing_UKTI_wp.pdf or http://www.eiu.com/CorporatePriorities2006

xvii David Livermore, Leading with Cultural Intelligence: The New Secret to Success AMACOM, 2010. 15.

xviii ibid.

xix Andy Andrews, The Butterfly Effect, Naperville, IL: Simple Truths, www. SimpleTruths.com, pp 11-53, 2009.

†† The Growing Leaders Career Ready Standards are based the Career Ready Practices, which are part of the Common Career Technical Core (www.careertech.org/CCTC <http://www. careertech.org/CCTC>). The Common Career Technical Core are wholly owned and the copyright held by the National Association of State Directors of Career Technical Education/ National Career Technical Education Foundation (NASDCTEc/NCTEF). Any use of these statements must be accompanied by the following copyright statement: "© Copyright 2012. National Association of State Directors of Career Technical Education/National Career Technical Education Foundation (NASDCTEc/NCTEF). All rights reserved."

ACKNOWLEDGMENTS

These *Habitudes* books are always a team effort. In many ways, this one is a giant illustration of the message in this book—it was the labor of multi-talented people who each invested their gifts, working as a team to see it through.

Thank you, Holly Moore, for your constant encouragement, added stories, valuable statistics, and for reading the manuscript through and making it better.

Thank you, Ashley Harzog and Kelli Garry, for doing research for this manuscript, filling folders with material that I could dig through for each chapter. I'm grateful.

Thank you to Brett Wilkes and Anne Alexander who edited and proofread this manuscript. I couldn't do a project like this without them.

Thank you, Jim Woodard, for your layout work making the content on these pages feel different than a textbook. I appreciate your willingness to be a lifelong learner.

Thank you Virginia Jackson and Levi Woodard for taking some of the photographs. Your creative flair makes these principles come to life.

Thank you, Andrea Callicott, for assisting me in all of my projects, ensuring I have the resources I need—including writing days to get the work done. I appreciate you.

Thank you, Jeff Gribble, for the cover design on each of these *Habitudes* books. You have an eye for what pops and what magnetically draws the eye. You're the best.

Finally, thank you to Rich Katt and Cory Epler who lead CTE efforts for the state of Nebraska. They had the original vision for this resource. Your friendship and foresight are invaluable.

[Notes]

[Notes]

[Notes]

HABITUDES®
IMAGES THAT FORM LEADERSHIP HABITS AND ATTITUDES

This book is all about helping students get ready for a career.

Developing employability skills has never been more important. In this ever-changing global economy, businesses all over the world want students who can enter a job with the ability to add value to the team, problem-solve, think critically, and communicate effectively. Unfortunately, a student could get an "A" in calculus, and not have those skills. We want to change that.

This book in the *Habitudes* series can help. Each of the images represent a skill employers have identified as critical to a person's success in a career. In this book, you'll discover the truth of:

- Surgeries and X-Rays
- Obstacle Course
- Bikes and Birds
- 3-D Glasses …and more

WHAT OTHERS ARE SAYING…

"No one teaches leadership better than Tim Elmore. This series is a must read."
– *John C. Maxwell*, author of *The 21 Irrefutable Laws of Leadership*

"*Habitudes* for Career Ready Students is an excellent 'vehicle' that supports our teachers as they help students master the Nebraska Career Readiness Standards. Our teachers say that the resources have challenged their students, helped them to think more critically, and truly helped them understand the key competencies behind the Nebraska Career Readiness Standards." - *Dr. Cory Epler, Deputy State Director of Career Education for the Nebraska Department of Education*

"My students love these images because they stick. I have heard conversations on our campus where the *Habitudes* keep coming up as practical reminders of how to do life."
– *Dr. Rex Bridges, High School Principal*

"The *Habitudes* images help us reinforce our mission, vision and values, and teach team members practical ways to personally own them in all of their actions." -*David McAnally, Jr., Vice President, Sales Training for LocumTenens.com (Jackson Healthcare)*

Dr. Tim Elmore is a recognized thought leader on understanding and connecting with the next generation. He is the author of more than 30 books, an international speaker, and the president of Growing Leaders. Growing Leaders is a non-profit organization committed to developing young leaders around the world to solve problems and serve people. You can learn more about Tim at:

www.GrowingLeaders.com

ISBN 978-0-9960783-5-1
51599>